Luscious Foods

Cooking with Fun & Style

Luscious Foods

Cooking with Fun & Style

Rudolf Sodamin

J & B EDITIONS

Dedication

To those people who love good food and presentation,
and to all culinary professionals
with whom I have had the pleasure of working.

J & B Editions, Inc.
891 Norfolk Square
Norfolk, VA 23502

Distributed by Hampton Roads Publishing Company, Inc.
891 Norfolk Square, Norfolk, Virginia 23502 (804)459-2453

Edited by Jan Carlton
Photographs supplied by and property of Rudolf Sodamin
Book and cover design by Jamie Raynor

Printed in the United States of America

Acknowledgements

In the course of writing *Luscious Foods,* I have been helped by a number of my colleagues whose patience, I am sure, I have often tried. I would especially like to thank my wife, Bente, for all her support and understanding; Joseph P. Smyth, Executive Vice President, Operations, Cunard Line, Lennart Hakanson, Senior Vice President Fleet Passenger Service, without whose help this book would never have been completed; and George Welser, my dear friend, who provided hours of his time to co-author my second cookbook.

I owe my grateful thanks to many people for their help and cooperation in writing my book; it would be impossible to mention everybody but I would like to mention the following for their continuous support:

To Susan Alpert to whom I wish a speedy and complete recovery, to Kjell Truedsson, Morton Mathiesen, Mike Smith, Olaug Strand, Linda Wright, Bernadette Doyle and Marge Espinet, David Morris, Ronald A. Santangelo, Priscilla Hoye, Judy Perl, Walter Meyer, and the Chairman of Cunard Line, Dermot St. J. McDermott.

My appreciation also to many of our talented Chefs de Cuisine onboard Queen Elizabeth 2, Vistafjord, Sagafjord and Sea Goddess I & II, young Chefs with outstanding talents and professionalism. Just to name a few who have given me valuable assistance in creating this book, Jonathan Wicks, Jeff Farnham, Bernhard Stumpfel, Freddy Schmidt, Jasmin Bin Saidun, Christian Carbrillet, Josef Reitstatter, Jackie Bellanger, Tony Milton, Karl Winkler, and Freddy Napotnick.

Special thanks to Morton Tadder of Tadder Associates for his eternal support.

Photographs by Herb Schmitz, London, England

Table of Contents

Foreword

Food is one of the most important features of the cruise ship experience. Passengers board a luxury cruise ship for an average of two weeks, and during this period have all their meals in the same dining room. In order to maintain passenger interest, the food has to not only taste good but also be visually stimulating.

Rudi Sodamin is a master in preparing and presenting fine foods. His talents are one of the reasons why 5 of the 10 Five-Star Plus cruise ships in the world sail under the Cunard banner.

Cunard is pleased to share his culinary talents with you. Meals that have delighted heads of state, heads of corporations, passengers with demanding tastes and passengers who just enjoy good food are recreated within the pages of *Luscious Foods*. I know that you will be fascinated by the variety of food presentations that Rudi has accumulated in his travels around the world.

It is our hope that this book gives you a taste of the cruise ship experience.

Joseph P. Smyth

Executive Vice President,
Operations
Cunard Line

Introduction

Dear Readers,

During my adolescence, I developed a taste for travel and a penchant for exploring new and exciting cuisines. Some years later, I made a decision to pursue a sea-going career which has enabled me to experience more of the world, but also to eat an assortment of different foods.

In my role as Corporate Executive Chef on board the QE2, I have been called upon many times to prepare lavish banquets and multiple course meals for such visiting luminaries as British and Japanese royalty, worldwide presidents of corporations and countries, and some of Hollywood's best-known celebrities. But most of all, I enjoy satisfying the palates of my special guests, the passengers.

Growing up in a large Austrian household, I was the fifth born of ten children. The unfortunate loss of our father during my early childhood left our mother to raise us single-handedly, fulfilling both parental roles. At the age of ten, I was delivering newspapers and doing odd jobs in neighborhood restaurants to help make ends meet. Being one of the eldest, I took it upon myself to help my mother in the kitchen preparing meals for the family. It was these difficult times and learning experiences that ultimately influenced my approach to cooking.

Meals prepared in our home were far from gourmet. However, my mother insisted on using only fresh vegetables and natural ingredients, and combining them with lots of love. We ate good, healthy, down-to-earth food. I remember it was always a joy to see my mother presenting one of her specialties to us at mealtime. Her simple but effective presentation of food has stayed with me throughout my years in cooking. And, in fact, I use this as a basis when I create my own dishes, at home and aboard ship. In my first cookbook, *The Cruise Ship Cookbook* (Little, Brown and Company, 1988), I made a point of emphasizing this basic concept of food preparation. My mother always used to say to me, "Besides trusting your sense of taste, use your eyes."

And to this day, successfully executed meals should not only taste good, but also be visually stimulating. In fact, the objective for writing *Luscious Foods* was inspired by producing attractive, eye-catching dishes and presenting foods that are simple to prepare—the very principle I credit to my mother.

I have presented *Luscious Foods* in a way to expand your culinary horizons—to turn ordinary looking food into dishes looking (and hopefully tasting) like those prepared by an accomplished chef. "The presentation of food should be joyful," I always remind my colleagues. "Think of cooking as a remarkable combination of aesthetics, interest, enthusiasm, and time. Use quality products and, most important of all, have patience".

It is my great hope and good wish that this book will inspire you to enjoy preparing meals with the right garnish so that your guests will think it took hours.

Bon Appetit,

Rudolf Sodamin
New York
Summer, 1991

Rudolf Sodamin

Vegetable Garnishes & Recipes

Artichokes

Fresh artichoke bottoms turn brown easily when exposed to air. Brushing the vegetable with lemon juice helps to eliminate this undesirable process. The bottoms may be filled with a variety of foods such as kiwi crowns, liver mousse, vegetable balls, turned vegetables, and truffled chicken mousse. Canned or cooked frozen artichoke bottoms may be used in place of the fresh and require less preparation.

To cook artichokes: Wash, trim stems, and remove loose outer leaves of artichokes. With a sharp knife, remove about 1 inch of the tops. Snip off sharp leaf tips. Brush cut surfaces with lemon juice. In a large heavy saucepan, cook artichokes in boiling salted water (cover well) about 20 to 30 minutes, or until leaf may be pulled from an artichoke easily. Place artichokes on absorbent paper, allowing them to drain well.

Note: 1 or 2 tablespoons lemon juice may be added to the cooking water, if desired.

Artichoke & Spinach "Flower" with Goose Liver

Yield: one "flower" motif or two to four hors d'oeuvres servings

5 ounces goose or chicken livers
2 teaspoons walnut oil
4 ounces spinach leaves, blanched
4 canned artichoke bottoms, drained and sliced
1 medium red bell pepper, finely cut julienne-style
1 to 2 teaspoons butter or margarine, melted
Chives, as needed
1 teaspoon minced black truffle
Madeira Sauce (see index)

In a small skillet, sauté goose or chicken livers in walnut oil over moderate heat until exterior is browned but interior remains a light pink; cut livers into bite-size pieces. Arrange spinach leaves (stems discarded) on a large platter in a circular flower shape. Arrange the artichoke slices on top of the spinach, each slice slightly overlapping the last one. Place the sautéed goose or chicken liver pieces in the center of the "flower" motif. Garnish chicken livers with thin strips of pepper (see photograph). Create "flower spikes", "leaves", and "stems", from chives (see photograph). Garnish center of "flower" with minced truffle. Serve with Madeira Sauce.

Artichokes with Trimmed Vegetables

*The secret of this garnish is to ensure that all the turned vegetables
are equal in size and length to give a more professional look.
This is an excellent vegetable accompaniment for roasted meats.*

Yield: two garnishes

2 artichoke bottoms,
  frozen or drained
  canned
1 carrot
1 small cucumber
1 zucchini
1 summer yellow
  squash
Boiling salted water,
  as needed
Ice water, as needed
2 to 3 firm radishes, as
  needed

Trim the artichoke bottoms to give a uniform appearance with a flat base. Peel carrots; using a sharp paring knife, cut carrots into equal lengths and then into quarters. Turn carrots (see index). Repeat process with cucumbers, zucchini, and yellow squash. In a medium heavy saucepan, blanch frozen artichoke bottoms, carrots, cucumber, zucchini, and yellow squash, uncovered, in salted boiling water for about 2 minutes or until vegetables are tender but crisp. Drain immediately and immerse in ice water (this process helps to conserve bright color). Drain vegetables well, patting lightly with absorbent paper. Arrange turned carrots, cucumber, zucchini, and yellow squash around side of artichoke bottoms, alternating colors and achieving a flower effect (see photograph).

With a sharp paring knife, thinly slice radishes. Place radish slices in a semicircle around the base of each artichoke bottom.

Note: Canned artichoke bottoms need no further cooking.

Carrot Fantasy

*To develop the composition of the fantasy floral arrangement,
the wooden skewers should be cut into different lengths.
Special care should also be given as to direction and scale,
just as in an arrangement of real flowers. To keep the arrangement
fresh, it should be sprayed with a mist of water
or kept in the refrigerator covered in plastic.*

Yield: about thirty "flowers"

2 medium carrots,
  peeled
2 to 3 radishes
  (optional)
1 very small
  yellow summer
  or zucchini
  squash (optional)
1 very small
  turnip (optional)
1 eggplant
About 30 long
  wooden skewers
Crisp curly
  endive (chicory),
  or other greens

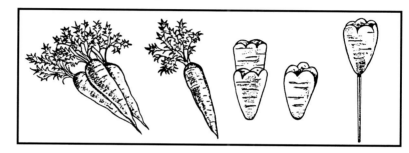

To prepare carrot buttercup "flowers", shape tip of carrots to delicately tapered cups. With a sharp knife, cut one "petal" about 1-inch from the tip and peeling down the tip, but leaving the "petal" intact. Continue cutting "petals" all the way around the tip. Gently twist the remaining top of the carrot to remove it from the newly formed "flower" cup. Reshape the tip and repeat cutting "flowers" from the carrot, until the entire carrot is used. "Flowers" may be left plain or contrasting centers may be added such as small round pieces of radish, squash, or turnip. Cut a thin slice lengthwise from the eggplant, allowing it to lay flat. Turn rounded side up. Cut wooden skewers to different lengths. Insert a skewer into the base of each "flower". Attach a contrasting center to the inside of each "flower" atop a skewer, if desired. Insert "flower" topped skewers in the center, gradually spacing each, with the shortest placed around the edge of the eggplant. Fill the base of the arrangement with curly endive or other greens to simulate greenery.

Cucumber "Drums"

Yield: about six to eight "drums" per cucumber

1 medium to large
   cucumber
2 radishes, sliced
   or coarsely chopped
Pitted black olives,
   as desired, sliced
   or coarsely chopped
Cream cheese, as
   desired, at room
   temperature
Mayonnaise, as desired
Seafood Mousse, as
   desired (see index)
Horseradish Cream,
   as desired (see index)
American Cocktail
   Seafood Sauce,
   as desired (see index)
Cherry tomatoes,
   as desired, each
   cut in half

Using a channel knife (see glossary of utensils), remove strips of skin lengthwise from top to bottom of cucumber, spaced at 1/2-inch intervals. Cut cucumber into 1-inch slices. Hollow out each slice with a spoon to form a shell. Edge may be cut decoratively into a zig-zag effect (see note). Fill "drums" as desired with sliced or chopped radishes or olives, combined with cream cheese or mayonnaise, if desired. Or, fill each with Seafood Mousse or Horseradish Cream or American Cocktail Seafood Sauce as desired. Garnish each with a cherry tomato half and a sprig of dill weed.

Note: To achieve a zig-zag or Van Dyke effect, cut small "Vs" around the edge of each cucumber slice by slowly rotating the slice and keeping the knife stationary.

Cucumber "Viking Boats"

These "Viking Boats" provide a most creative display to enhance
any food presentation. They may be filled with any variety
of vegetables, coleslaw, melon balls, chicken salad,
or Waldorf Salad, or other foodstuff.

Yield: four "boats"

5 medium cucumbers, blemish-free
4-inch wooden skewers, as needed (about 8 to 10 per "boat")
About 4 to 8 cherry tomatoes
About 4 to 8 pitted black olives, drained
About 4 to 8 radishes
1 red bell pepper, cored, seeded, and cut into small squares

Starting 1 to 2 inches from either end, cut a thick slice (about one-fourth of the cucumber) vertically from the cucumber; scoop out the seeds and flesh, leaving a shell or "boat" (see photograph). Fill "boat" as desired. Insert 4 to 5 wooden skewers into each side of the "boat", extending outward to simulate oars. Fashion the cut-away slice into two long oval pieces; insert a skewer through each and attach vertically to center of "boat" as a "sail" (see photograph). Repeat process three times more. Thinly slice remaining cucumber. Alternately thread 4 skewers with a cucumber slice, cherry tomato, olive, radish, and a pepper square; insert a vegetable threaded skewer vertically into one end of each "boat".

Cucumber "Dragon"

Kids will love whimsical Magnus the Dragon

Yield: one "dragon" centerpiece

1 to 2 green
  onions
Ice water,
  as needed
A few ice cubes
1 medium
  to large
  cucumber
1 medium
  carrot, peeled
  and thinly
  sliced
  crosswise
1 cherry tomato
Short wooden
  picks, as
  needed
A few artichoke
  leaves,
  blanched, for
  the "head"
1 radish, or
  pimento-
  stuffed olive,
  thinly sliced
1 teaspoon
  cream cheese,
  at room
  temperature,
  or mayonniase,
  or sour cream
2 capers, drained
2 or 3 long thin
  red bell pepper
  strips

Very thinly cut green onions at each end, bulb and leaves, each cut about 1/2 to 3/4-inch in length, to make a frilled "tail". Immerse onions in ice water to which a few ice cubes have been added; cover in clear plastic wrap and refrigerate for several hours to allow "tails" to open and frills to curl. With a sharp knife, make a vertical cut, about 1 to 1 1/2-inches in length, in one end of the cucumber to form the "dragon's mouth". Cut 1/4-inch thick slices crosswise, about three fourths of the way through, in remaining portion of cucumber, allowing slices to remain intact. Insert carrot slices into cuts in the cucumber to form the "dragon's feet". Turn cucumber over, carrot side down. Insert cherry tomato into the mouth of the "dragon" and secure with two wooden picks. Arrange a few blemish-free artichoke leaves on "dragon's head", securing with wooden picks (see photograph). Arrange 2 radish slices on "dragon's face" above mouth; dot each with a spot of cream cheese, mayonnaise, or sour cream and then top with capers to give a realistic look (see photograph). Drain frilled onions and insert into cucumber end opposite head. Garnish the back of the "dragon" with red bell pepper strips held in place with dabs of mayonnaise. Arrange "dragon" on a serving tray or display board. Surround with food of choice.

Fennel "Barrow"

Children and adults will appreciate the whimsical fennel barrow.

Yield: three "barrows"

1 stalk fennel
Lemon juice
  as needed
1 small carrot,
  peeled
3 (4-inch)
  wooden
  skewers
Grapes, olives,
  or vegetable
  julienne of
  choice

Clean fennel thoroughly, removing all sand and grit. With a sharp knife, remove two-thirds of the stalk from the top, leaving the "handle" of the "barrow", and leafy end. Cut diagonally from the stalk through to the bulb; remove fennel layers (see photograph). Sprinkle fennel with lemon juice to prevent it from turning brown. Cut the carrot crosswise into 1/2-inch thick slices. Attach a carrot slice at the end of a 4-inch wooden skewer; insert the skewer, opposite end, through the bulb of the fennel. Attach a carrot slice to free end of skewer. Repeat process for 3 "barrows". Fill "barrows" with grapes, olives, or vegetable julienne of choice.

Fennel Stuffed with Sour Cream and Berries or Waldorf Salad

*This garnish is perfect with cold chicken or turkey
and will brighten up any summer lunch.*

Yield: garnish for two servings

1 head (small to medium) fennel (about 4 to 5 ribs per head)
Lemon juice, as needed
2 cups sour cream or cottage cheese
8 to 10 blueberries
2 strawberries, hulled and cleaned
2 raspberries
2 small sprigs of mint
Waldof Salad (see index)
4 seedless orange segments
4 cherry tomatoes
2 English walnut halves

Trim root from fennel head. Carefully remove ribs, leaving feathery green leaves in place. Reserve center part for other use. Rinse in water to which lemon juice has been added to prevent discoloration of fennel. With a sharp knife, cut the base of each fennel rib on a slant, allowing each rib to stand upright. Using a pastry/piping bag with a 5 star-shaped nozzle, fill bag with sour cream and pipe into each rib. Arrange 2 blueberries, a strawberry, and a raspberry on each sour cream filled fennel rib and garnish each with a sprig of mint. Or, fill each prepared fennel rib with Waldorf Salad. Garnish each entrée serving with a Waldorf Salad filled fennel rib. Arrange an orange segment, a cherry tomato, and a walnut half on each filled fennel rib. Be careful fennel rib is in proportion to plate.

Note: Fennel may be blanched before using, if desired. In a medium, heavy saucepan, bring water to boiling. Add fennel and cook for 1 minute or until tender but crisp; remove fennel immediately, draining well. Refresh in ice cold water to retain color.

Waldorf Salad

Yield: garnish for four servings

1 apple, peeled and chopped
1/2 cup chopped English walnuts
1/4 cup mayonnaise or sour cream
1/2 teaspoon lemon juice
Salt and white pepper to taste

In a medium bowl, combine apple, celery, and walnuts. Add mayonnaise or sour cream, lemon juice, and salt and pepper to taste, mixing well.

Onion Lotus "Flowers"

Lotus are flowers used widely in Asia, especially in religious ceremonies. Representing purity, the lotus vary in color from white to light pink. Choose cervical shaped onions with one bulb centers to achieve the best flower effect. The onion should be peeled, but the base should not be cut as the "flower" will fall apart. Arrange onion lotus and pepper lilies in a bouquet or as individual flowers.

Yield: one "lotus" arrangement

4 medium Bermuda or Spanish onions
Ice water, as needed
2 medium red bell peppers
Long wooden skewers as needed
1 medium cabbage half, or 1 large potato, unpeeled
12 sprigs crisp curly endive (chicory), or other greens

Remove peel from each onion, being careful not to cut the base. Using a sharp small knife, make a zig-zag cut around the center of the onion through the first onion layer; remove cut away portion. Continue cutting away, layer by layer, toward one end of the onion, until the center layer is reached (see illustration). Repeat process with all onions. Immerse onions in ice water to allow onions to become firm. Cut the red peppers vertically into long pieces, about 1/2- inch wide. Remove core and stem, but do not remove seeds and pulp. Immerse pepper strips in ice water. Insert wooden picks into the base of the onions and pepper strips and then insert "flower" topped picks into cabbage half or potato. Follow floral arranging instructions for Carrot Fantasy (see index). Fill the base of the arrangement with sprigs of curly endive or other greenery.

Bell Pepper "Flowers"

*These "flowers" may be laid out on a plate as a display or used
to decorate food. With a little imagination, one can create a unique design.
There is a bounty of food which can be turned into an artistic display creation.
The ingredients may further be used to prepare a tasty vegetable soup
after the display is completed.*

Yield: a bouquet (about six)

1 medium red
bell pepper
1 medium green
bell pepper
1 medium yellow
bell pepper
1 bunch
watercress
1 pitted black
olive, drained
Cooked white
of an egg
3 medium car-
rots, peeled
1 zucchini
1 yellow summer
squash
1 white turnip,
peeled
Few green peas,
blanched (see
note)

With a sharp knife, cut red and yellow peppers
into thin rings and green pepper into thin strips.
Use rings for "flower petals" and strips for "flower
stems". Cut small rounds from cooked egg white
to also form "flower centers". Peas and olives can
also be used as centers for "flowers". Use watercress leaves as "leaves" of the "flowers". With a
melon baller, scoop out balls from carrots, zucchini, yellow squash, and turnip to use as "flower
bed". Arrange an attractive floral design as desired
with prepared vegetables (see photograph) on a
service platter or display board.

*Note: Cook fresh peas in boiling salted water for 3 to
4 minutes; refresh immediately in ice water to pre-
serve color. Frozen peas need not be blanched. Do not
use canned peas.*

Medley of Peppers

Pepper flowers are large. Care must be given in the design to eliminate them overwhelming an arrangement. Generally they are displayed in the center of an hors d'oeuvre platter.

Yield: one arrangement, about six to eight pepper "flowers"

1 medium yellow
  bell pepper
1 medium red bell
  pepper
1 medium orange
  bell pepper
1 medium green
  bell pepper
Ice water
2 red cabbage
  leaves
5 radishes
About 30 (8 to 10-
  inch) wooden
  skewers
1 large eggplant
1 bunch of thyme

Remove the top and bottom of each pepper. Cut each pepper into 3 equal-size large squares; discard core, seeds, and pulp. Using a sharp knife, outline a heart shape in each. Immerse pepper pieces in ice water. Refrigerate for 8 to 48 hours to allow pepper pieces to curl. Peppers require extra time to open. Cut cabbage leaves into long slender strands. Immerse in ice water also. Allow wooden skewers to soak in a second bowl of water to become pliable. Cut about 5 to 6 *very* small balls out of the radishes. Cut a thin slice lengthwise from one side of the eggplant; turn eggplant rounded side up. Drain peppers. Insert a skewer into the underneath side of each pepper piece. Attach a radish ball to top of each pepper piece, securing to attached skewers. Insert pepper "flowers" into eggplant base, longer skewers arranged toward the center of the base. Skewer the red cabbage in the same manner as the pepper pieces and then insert into the eggplant between the pepper pieces. Garnish the base with thyme.

Bell Pepper Shells Filled with Vegetables

Bell peppers are versatile vegetables with many uses. They come in many colors, including red, yellow, orange, purple, and green.

Yield: four pepper shells, one per serving

2 large green, red, or yellow bell peppers
1/2 cup broccoli florets or spears, blanched (see note)
1/2 cup cauliflower florets, blanched (see note)
1 small head Belgian endive, cleaned, core removed, and separated into leaves
1 small head radicchio, cleaned, core removed, separated into leaves
4 to 8 ears baby corn
1/2 cup cocktail *(very small)* onions, drained

With a sharp knife, cut peppers in half lengthwise; remove core, seeds, and white pulp. Peppers may be left raw or blanched in boiling salted water for about 2 minutes. Drain immediately and refresh in ice water. Fill peppers with broccoli florets or spears, cauliflower florets, Belgian endive leaves, radicchio leaves, baby corn, cocktail onions or a combination of vegetables. Or, fill with any prepared vegetable or salad recipe desired.

Note: Cook broccoli and cauliflower in boiling salted water until just tender but crisp; drain immediately and refresh in ice water to retain fresh color.

Kiwi Star Filled with Strawberry Foam

Chock full of vitamins and flavor, kiwi is a versatile fruit, which has become popular in the United States in the past few years. It can be cut in a star design and garnished with Fruit Foam or cream cheese and finished with a fruit slice as shown in the photograph.

Baby Potato Shells

Yield: four servings

12 to 16 *very small firm* potatoes
Hot cooking oil, as needed (optional)
Butter or margarine, at room temperature, as needed
Salt and pepper to taste
Julienne of cooked mixed vegetables (optional)
Florets of cooked broccoli and/or cauliflower (optional)
Cooked onion "fans" (optional) (see index for Onion Lotus "Flowers")

Cut each potato in half crosswise. Using a sharp paring knife, trim the bottom of each half so that it stands upright with a flat underneath surface (see note). Hollow out each potato half to form a shell with a spoon or Parisienne scoop (see glossary of utensils); reserve the scooped out portion to cook separately, if desired. Cook potato shells in boiling salted water for about 15 minutes or until *just* fork tender. *Do not overcook.* Or, deep-fry potato shells in 3 to 4-inches of hot oil (375 degrees F.) until golden brown. Cook the scooped out potato in boiling salted water for about 15 to 20 minutes or until fork tender and easy to mash; drain well. With a potato masher or electric beaters, mash or purée potatoes. Add butter as desired and salt and pepper to taste. Fill cooked potato shells with seasoned puréed potatoes or julienne of cooked mixed vegetables, cooked broccoli and/or cauliflower florets, or cooked onions. May reheat in a very slow oven (275 degrees F.) for a few minutes as needed before serving.

Note: Potato shells which are deep-fried should be peeled first.

Mashed Potato Based Shapes

Yield: about three to four servings

2 cups mashed potatoes
  (see note)
2 egg yolks, lightly
  beaten
Salt and pepper to taste
Pinch of nutmeg
Flour, as needed
2 eggs, beaten
Breadcrumbs, as needed
Whole cloves, as needed
Crushed blanched
  almonds
Uncooked spaghetti
  strands, cut into
  1 1/2-inch pieces,
  as needed
Hot cooking oil
Sprigs of mint

In a bowl, combine potatoes, egg yolks, salt, pepper, and nutmeg, mixing well. To prepare Potato Duchesse, fit a pastry/piping bag with a medium star-shaped nozzle. Fill bag with potato mixture; pipe mixture into 6 equal-size circular mounds, making each circle smaller at the top of each potato mound, spaced 2 inches apart, onto a greased baking sheet. Bake in a hot oven (400 degrees F.) for 7 to 8 minutes or until golden brown.

Note: The potato mixture may also be piped into equal-size nest shapes, each with a center cavity, baked, and then filled with diced tomatoes, cubed cooked vegetables, or a bouquet of cooked small whole vegetables.

Potato Croquettes: Form potato mixture into equal-size small cylinder or sausage shapes, each about 3 to 4 inches in length. Dredge each croquette in flour, coating lightly, then dip each in beaten eggs, and finally roll each in bread crumbs, coating well. Deep-fry in hot oil (about 3 to 4 inches, 375 degrees F.) until golden brown.

Almond Balls: Prepare as in croquettes, but form potato mixture into small balls. Dredge each ball in flour, then dip in beaten egg mixture, and roll in crushed almonds, coating well. Deep-fry as previously directed.

Pear/Apple-Shaped Croquettes: Roll potato mixture into balls, using the thumb and first two fingers, taper off the top part and flatten the bottom of each ball to form a pear shape. Insert a 1 1/2-inch piece of spaghetti into tapered end and a clove into the middle of base end. For apple shapes, make an indentation into tapered end where spaghetti is inserted. Complete as previously directed.

Potato Nests

Potato Nests is a highly stylized, but easy-to-do, fail-proof presentation which can be served with roasts such as venison and beef. Most any small food stuff may be used to fill the nests. They make an attractive addition to any serving plate.

Yield: two nests

1 firm large potato
Hot cooking oil, as needed
Sprigs of basil, oregano, thyme, rosemary, cilantro, chervil, or any herb of choice for garnish (optional)
Assorted small vegetable balls for garnish (optional)
Assorted fruit pieces for garnish (optional)

Peel potatoes and *immediately* immerse in cold water to cause potatoes to become pliable and prevent discoloration. Using a mandoline (see glossary of cooking utensils) or a sharp zig-zag knife, thinly slice potatoes. Arrange potato slices at the bottom of a nest basket (see glossary of cooking utensils), being sure the slices all touch or overlap each other. The potato slices must be arranged in this manner as the starch content in the potatoes will cause them to stick together to hold the nest shape when cooked. Clamp basket top in place and deep-fry in hot oil (375 to 400 degrees F.) for 3 to 4 minutes or until golden brown. Drain well.

When potato nest is cooled, open basket carefully; separate potato nest from basket by tapping basket lightly with a knife. Repeat process until all potato slices are used. Garnish each basket by filling with sprigs of desired herbs or small vegetable balls or small pieces of fruit. Most any small edible foodstuff may be used to fill the nests.

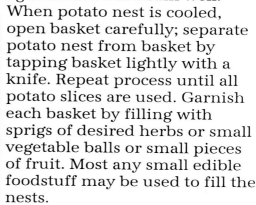

Variation: Peeled carrots or turnips or parsnips or the bulb or base of a celery stalk may be thinly sliced and used in place of the potato slices.

Harvest Pumpkin

*The Harvest Pumpkin makes a beautiful salad presentation.
As an alternative, the pumpkin may be used as a punch bowl
or as a soup tureen. It is an ideal recipe to serve guests
during the Autumn/Winter holiday season.*

Yield: about twelve to fourteen servings

1 large pumpkin, about 8 to 10-pounds
6 kiwi
4 firm, medium bananas
Lemon juice as needed
4 medium apples
2 papaya (see note)
1 medium pine-apple
2 pounds seedless, black or green grapes
1 quart strawber-ries, cleaned and hulled
Grand Marnier or other liqueur of choice as desired (see note)
Sugar water (see note)

With a sharp knife, cut the pumpkin in half around its middle in a zig-zag pattern. Scoop out the pulp, seeds, and most of the flesh, leaving a shell with a thin inner layer of pumpkin flesh; reserve top for a lid. Prepare scooped out flesh for other use as desired; discard pulp and seeds. Peel and cut bananas into thin slices; immediately sprinkle liberally with lemon juice to maintain banana's color. Remove core and seeds from apples; peel if desired. Cut apples into bite-sized pieces; immediately sprinkle with lemon juice. Peel papaya and pineapple; cut into cubes. Arrange fruits in bottom pumpkin shell; sprinkle liberally with Grand Marnier or other liqueur and sugar water. Arrange lid slightly askew atop pumpkin.

Note: Two cantaloupe may be used in place of papaya if papaya is not available.

Note: Orange juice may be used in place of liqueur.

Note: Sugar water may be prepared by combining equal parts of sugar and water in a saucepan; i.e. 1 cup of each. Boil for 5 minutes over high heat, then allow mixture to cool.

Variation of Radish Cutting

*The radish is a salad vegetable of crisp and crunchy texture,
displaying two dominant colors. With the deft use of a knife,
many attractive designs can be made.*

*By cutting around the mid-section of the radish or by gouging,
a "U" shaped "flower petal" is formed. These must be left in ice water
to allow the "petals" to open. A mushroom shape can be achieved
by cutting one-third of the radish away, leaving a "stem"
extending from the center.*

Radish "Mice"

For a delightful accent to a cheese board, celebrate with Radish Mice.

**Yield: sixteen radish "mice",
about twelve to sixteen appetizer servings**

16 large radishes
48 whole cloves or
  black pepper-
  corns
1 pound Swiss
  cheese or other
  desired cheese
Sprigs of parsley,
  chervil, or
  watercress

Wash radishes; dry thoroughly on absorbent paper. Remove any leaves from radishes; allow threadlike root to remain intact. Cut a thin slice from the side of the radish, allowing it to stand firm; reserve cut portion for "ears". Cut reserved piece of radish into two pieces. With a sharp small knife, cut two notches on either side of the radish at end opposite root or "tail". Insert a radish piece into each notch to form "ears". Insert two cloves or peppercorns into the radish below the "ears" to form "eyes" and the "nose" (see photograph). Repeat process until all "mice" are completed. Arrange mice over and around a block or slices of Swiss or other desired cheese. Garnish with sprigs of parsley, chervil, or watercress.

Scatter Radish Mice over a cheese board with some mustardcress or watercress for a unique and humorous touch.

Red Radish Galore

*Radish "Buttercups" can be arranged to form a centerpiece
to be used as a table decoration for any buffet or cocktail reception.
Attention needs to be given to the scale of the arrangement,
as well as its overall composition.*

Yield: one centerpiece

12 medium radishes
2 to 3 medium carrots, peeled
12 (8 to 10-inch) wooden skewers
1 medium cucumber
1 medium turnip
Curly endive or other crisp greens as needed

With a sharp paring knife, cut about 4 to 5 rounded petal shapes around the edge of a radish (see drawing). Gently twist the center of the radish and remove from the newly formed "flower" cup. Repeat process to form "flowers" from remaining radishes. Soak radish "flowers" in ice water to cover in the refrigerator for several hours. Using a Parisienne scoop (see glossary of cooking terms), form 12 balls from the carrots; soak in ice water to cover in the refrigerator for several hours. Allow skewers to soak in water for several hours to become pliable. To form a "floral arrangement", attach a radish "flower", securing on the tip of each skewer. Cut a *very thin* slice from the turnip and cucumber to form flat bases. Arrange bases on a platter or display board. Insert "flower" topped skewers into the turnip and cucumber bases, dividing as desired. Arrange sprigs of curly endive or other greens around the base of the skewers to simulate floral greenery.

Note: Arrangement may be prepared 24 hours in advance, misted, covered, and refrigerated.

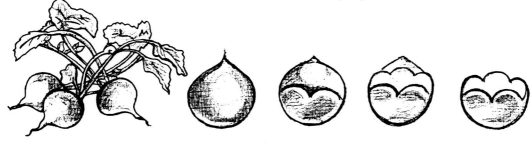

East Meets West

East Meets West is the epitome of presentations.
As the photograph illustrates, there are unique ways
in a variety of styles which can be mixed
to create an overall display to accent entrée plates.

Included in the photograph clockwise from 10 o'clock:

* *Yellow squash with radish center.*
* *Yellow bell pepper filled with broccoli and cauliflower florets, bell*
  pepper strips, and a small Belgian endive.
* *Green bell pepper filled with symmetrically sliced cucumbers, yellow*
  and red bell pepper, and peeled carrots, as well as cauliflower
  florets.
* *Tomato stuffed with a bouquet of turned vegetables.*
* *Tomato stuffed with florets of cauliflower and broccoli.*
* *Fennel half stuffed with assorted stuffed vegetables.*
* *Along, large white radish formed into an "eel" or "fish"*
  accented with a turned zucchini "head" and "face" and a strip
  of red bell pepper for the "tongue" and whole cloves for the "eyes".

Variation of Tomatoes

Tomatoes used as a garnish or decoration are attractive eye catchers.
The photograph displays a variety of shapes and sizes . . . petite baby tomatoes
as well as normal sized ones . . . wedges, halves, and whole tomatoes . . .
filled with an assortment of foodstuffs. Fantasy and creation
join in preparation of these crowd pleasers.

Cherry Tomato "Mice"

*For an attractive presentation, place mice on a block of Swiss cheese
with some of the mice peering out from the holes.*

Yield: sixteen tomato "mice"

16 cherry tomatoes
48 whole cloves or
    black peppercorns
16 radish roots or
    long thin pliable
    twigs
1 pound Swiss or
    other desired
    cheese
Sprigs of parsley,
    chervil, or
    watercress

With a sharp knife, cut a *very thin* slice from side of each cherry tomato. Loosen skin from rounded end opposite stem; roll back skin, slitting in the center, to form ears. Insert cloves or peppercorns into tomato flesh where skin has been rolled back to form "eyes" and a "nose" for each "mouse". Repeat process until all "mice" are completed. Arrange "mice" around a block or slices of Swiss or other desired cheese. Garnish with sprigs of parsley, chervil, or watercress.

Petite Plum or Pear Shaped Tomatoes

Plum or pear shaped tomatoes are just one of the many varieties of tomatoes available. Named for their shape, these tomatoes have an excellent flavor and keep well. They are good for preserving and serving in salads. As shown in the photograph, they are a visual delight and make an impressive garnish. Whole cloves and mint complement the simple design.

One Half "Winged" Tomato

Yield: one garnish

1 firm ripe
tomato
Sprig of
parsley

With a sharp small knife, remove the stem scar of the tomato. Turn tomato rounded side up. Make a large deep "V" shape incision into the tomato. Repeat this process two to three times more, making each incision smaller and less deep. Gently push the "V" cuts away from the base of the tomato to create a winged effect. Garnish with a sprig of parsley. The garnish may be cut in advance, but the last two steps should be done *just* before using to prevent the tomato from wilting and looking unappetizing.

Tomato Stuffed with Tomato Mousse

Yield: two servings or six entrée garnishes

1 firm large tomato
2 tablespoons minced peeled onion
1 teaspoon butter or margarine, melted
3 tablespoons tomato paste
1 teaspoon minced fresh or 1/4 to 1/2 teaspoon dried basil, oregano, thyme, or dill weed
1 tablespoon unflavored gelatin
1 1/2 tablespoons cold water
Salt and pepper to taste
1 medium zucchini
2 hard cooked quail eggs for garnish, peeled (optional) (see note)
Bits of black truffle for garnish (optional)
Pimento-stuffed green or pitted black olives for garnish

Remove stem scar in top of tomato. With a sharp knife, cut tomato in half crosswise. Scoop out pulp and seeds; set aside. Turn tomato shells upside down to drain thoroughly; dry inside of shells thoroughly with absorbent paper. If cherry tomatoes are used, cut a *very thin* slice from the top of each tomato, then scoop pulp and seeds from each.

In a small heavy skillet, sauté onions in butter over moderate heat until onions are tender but not browned; stir in reserved tomato pulp and continue cooking for about 2 minutes. Add tomato paste and herbs, blending well. Cook for another minute.

In a 1-cup measure, sprinkle gelatin over cold water; blend thoroughly. Add to tomato mixture, stirring until gelatin is completely dissolved. Season mixture with salt and pepper to taste. Pour mixture into a blender container; cover and whiz at medium speed until mixture is puréed. Pour into a small glass bowl and refrigerate until *just* firm.

Fill tomato shells with tomato mousse. Or, fill a pastry/piping bag fitted with a nozzle with mousse and pipe into tomato shells. Chill until ready to serve. Garnish each serving with a quail egg and a bit of black truffle. Or, garnish each serving with pimento-stuffed green or pitted black olives. Use mousse filled cherry tomatoes as entrée garnishes.

Note: Quail eggs are available in many specialty food shops.

Stuffed Tomatoes with Vegetables

A variety of ingredients such as green beans, hearts of palm, asparagus spears, carrot sticks, or broccoli florets may be used to fill tomatoes to produce a colorful and appetizing effect.

Yield: four garnishes

4 medium
tomatoes
8 ounces
green beans
1 leek

With a sharp knife, cut a *very thin* slice from the bottom of each tomato so that it will stand firmly erect. Then cut about one-third from the top of each tomato. Using a Parisienne scoop (see glossary of utensils) or a teaspoon, remove all the pulp and seeds from each. Trim green beans, each to about 3 inches in length. Blanch the beans and leek in boiling salted water (beans for about 3 to 4 minutes and leek for *only* 30 to 60 seconds); drain and refresh in ice water. Cut the leek into small strips and then tie the beans into attractive bundles with the strips, arranging the leek strips into bows. Arrange green bean bundles in each tomato shell.

Tomato Stuffed with Tuna Cream Cheese or Chicken Liver Mousse

This garnish or luncheon entrée is very simple and quick to prepare. The ingredients used such as a fish or vegetable mousse or duxelles can provide spectacular results. For a dramatic presentation, cut out a quarter of the tomato as shown in the photograph and fill as desired.

Yield: two servings

2 ounces albacore tuna, drained
1/2 ounce cream cheese, at room temperature
1/4 ounce blue or Roquefort cheese at room temperature
About 2 teaspoons lemon juice
Salt and pepper to taste
Minced parsley for garnish
Chicken Liver Mousse (see index)
2 small to medium tomatoes

Combine tuna, cream cheese, and blue or Roquefort cheese in the container of a blender or food processor; cover and whiz or process until mixture is smooth. Add lemon juice and salt and pepper to taste, mixing well. Chill mixture while preparing tomatoes. Blanch tomatoes in boiling salted water for about 10 seconds, *just* until skin breaks or blisters and breaks; drain immediately and refresh in ice water. Peel away skin and remove stem scars from tomatoes. Cut off a thin slice from the top and a *very thin* slice from the base of each tomato; scoop out the flesh and seeds, leaving two tomato shells. Cut a wedge out of each tomato, leaving the wedge intact at the tomato base (see photograph). Fill one or both tomatoes with tuna mixture or Chicken Liver Mousse as desired, allowing to spill over onto tomato wedge as shown in photograph.

Vegetable "Boats"

Vegetable "Boats" may be used to complement large roasts. Serve warm or at room temperature. They also may be served as a raw or cooked vegetable hors d'oeuvre accompanied with Yogurt Dill Sauce.

Yield: three "boats"

1 medium to large zucchini

1 medium to large yellow summer squash

1 medium to large cucumber

1 carrot, peeled

1 turnip, peeled

1 potato, peeled

1/2 cup broccoli florets

1/2 cup cauliflower florets

3 to 4 radishes, trimmed

3 to 4 pitted black olives, drained

Sprigs of fresh chives, thyme, and basil

Yogurt Dill Sauce (optional), (see index)

With a sharp knife, cut a thin slice lengthwise from each of the zucchini, yellow squash, and cucumber. Hollow out each with a Parisienne scoop (see glossary of utensils) or spoon, forming dug-out "boats". A zig-zag or scalloped edge may be fashioned, if desired. Cut carrot, turnip, and potato into uniform small barrel shapes; blanch in boiling salted water, drain well, and refresh immediately in ice water. Cut radishes on 4 sides to form petal shapes, leaving intact at stem end; refresh in ice water. Garnish each vegetable "boat" with an assortment of vegetables, olives, and herbs. Serve with Yogurt Dill Sauce.

Bouquet of Turned Vegetables

Turned vegetables may be served lightly sautéed with any main course or entrée. As shown in this photograph, they may also be used as an attractive edible decoration for a buffet table. To retain the color of the vegetables, they must be blanched for about three minutes in boiling salted water and then immediately refreshed by immersing in ice water.

Vegetable Curls

*Vegetable Curls make attractive strip flowers which can be used
effectively to garnish salad platters, roasted meats, and many fish recipes.*

Yield: one flower per piece of vegetable

Leeks, green
  onions, chili
  peppers, celery
  ribs, as desired,
  cut into 1 1/2 to
  4-inch pieces
Ice water
Ice cubes or
  crushed ice

Using a sharp knife, cut thin strips from top
to bottom of leeks, green onions, chili peppers
and celery pieces, leaving one end of each intact.
In a deep bowl, immerse vegetables in ice water
to which several ice cubes or crushed ice have
been added. Refrigerate for several hours until
vegetables curl (see photograph).

"*Vegetable Garden*"

*This attractive "vegetable garden" requires patience and imagination.
It could be used to enhance the visual appeal of poached whole salmon,
turkey, chicken, roast beef or pâté coated in Chaud Froid
and served on a buffet table.*

Yield: one vegetable display

2 carrots
1 cucumber
1 leek
1 lemon
1 egg white
1/2 teaspoon
   vinegar
3 tomato roses
   (see index)
Aspic for
   glazing
   (see index)

In a medium heavy saucepan, blanch carrots, cucumber, leek, and lemon for about 2 minutes; immediately drain and refresh in ice water. Poach egg white in simmering water to which vinegar has been added for about 5 to 6 minutes; drain well. Peel carrots and thinly slice crosswise. Thinly slice cucumber crosswise. Thinly slice leek into leaf shapes. With a vegetable peeler, remove peel of lemon in one long piece. Cut carrot slices and cucumber slices into "petal" shapes. Cut lemon peel into a round shape to represent the sun with thin strips for "rays". Cut poached egg white into "petal" and "flower" center shapes as well as "cloud"

shapes. Prepare tomato "roses". Arrange shaped vegetables and egg white into desired display (see photograph). Brush display with aspic to enhance its appearance and prevent display from drying out.

Luscious Foods

Lavishly Displayed Vegetable Platters

*These beautiful presentations of vegetables
are similar to presentations used
to garnish buffets served on the Queen Elizabeth 2.*

Carrot sticks wrapped in leeks
Artichoke bottoms filled
** with vegetable balls**
Turned mushrooms
Leek stalks
Turned vegetables
Artichoke hearts
Ring of cucumber fans

Artichoke bottoms with
** broccoli spears**
Tomato roses
Green (spring) onions
Cucumber wedges with
** cauliflower roses**
Carrot, zucchini, and
** turnip balls**
Yellow squash

"Hen" of Zucchini and Bell Peppers

This fanciful centerpiece will brighten any platter of food.

Yield: one centerpiece

1 medium to
large zucchini,
for "neck of
body"
1 medium
eggplant,
for base
Wooden picks
as needed
1 medium red
bell pepper
1 medium green
bell pepper
1 medium
yellow bell
pepper
1 small carrot for
"beak", peeled
and cut into
beak shape
Sprigs of
rosemary or
thyme

With a sharp knife, cut a thin slice horizontally from one side of eggplant so that it will stand firm, rounded side turned up. Cut a thin slice from the underside or bottom end opposite the stem of the zucchini, so that it will stand firmly on the eggplant base. Attach zucchini securely to eggplant, at end opposite stem with wooden picks (see photograph). Remove core and seeds from peppers; cut peppers into slender oval shapes, similar to feathers. Attach pepper strips to zucchini with wooden picks (see photograph). Fasten carrot piece to zucchini to form a "beak", securing with wooden picks (see photograph). Garnish "tail" area and eggplant base with sprigs of rosemary or thyme (see photograph).

Rudolf Sodamin

Fruit Garnishes & Recipes

Various Apple Garnishes

*Apples can be made into charming garnishes to accent starters,
main courses, and desserts. Different shapes and colors
of the fruit add visual interest.*

Apple Baskets

Refer to instructions for Lemon Baskets (see index). Substitute an apple for the lemon, taking care not to snap off the handle. Soak in or sprinkle apple liberally with lemon juice to prevent discoloration of fruit. Carefully fill with strawberry slices or halved raspberries or blueberries and garnish with a sprig of mint. The following garnishes may be used collectively to dress a main dish or individual serving plates.

* Cut an apple into quarters. Soak apple quarters in lemon juice and then thinly slice lengthwise, removing core and seeds. Arrange slices in a semicircle. Apple may be used raw or slightly cooked, as desired

* Cut apple in half. Using a medium size ring, cut out a circle from each half. Sprinkle each with lemon juice. Place a peeled slice of kiwi on each apple circle. Garnish each with a Maraschino cherry.

* Cut apple in half; peel, trim, and sprinkle each half with lemon juice. Arrange orange segments and a Maraschino cherry half on each half in a flower design.

* Cut apple in half; peel, trim and sprinkle each half with lemon juice. Arrange 3 orange segments and 3 peeled kiwi segments on each apple half, alternating orange segments and kiwi slices. Garnish each with a strawberry *fleur de lis* (sliced almost through with slices spread to form a "fan" shape).

* With a sharp knife, cut apple into a square. Using a Parisienne cutter (see glossary of utensils), scoop out the inside of the box; soak or sprinkle liberally with lemon juice. Fill with blueberries and garnish with a vine leaf.

* With a sharp knife, cut the apple in a zig-zag shape, Van Dyke-style (see index). Soak in or sprinkle liberally with lemon juice. Using a Parisienne cutter, scoop out the inside of the apple. Fill apple with a Van Dyke-cut kiwi and garnish with raspberries.

Apple "Stars" on a Tomato Base

This garnish is ideal with roast beef, as well as roast turkey or chicken.

Yield: one garnish

1 firm medium
  tomato
1 medium apple
Lemon juice, as
  needed
Slice of black olive,
  for garnish
Maraschino cherry
  half, drained, for
  garnish

With a sharp knife, cut a thin slice from the top and bottom of the tomato to allow it to stand firmly upright. Cut apple horizontally into 2 slices, removing core and seeds. Sprinkle apple slices liberally with lemon juice to prevent discoloration of fruit. Using a star cutter, cut out 2 star shapes from the apple. Place the trimmed tomato on top of one apple "star"; top tomato with second tomato "star". Arrange a black olive slice over hole in apple slice; top olive with Maraschino cherry half.

Note: Smaller garnishes may be prepared using cherry tomatoes and a smaller star cutter.

Avocado Filled with Fruit Salad

An avocado half filled with an assortment of fruits provides a visually attractive
but easy to prepare luncheon entrée or display presentation. Choose
a firm ripe avocado; cut in half lengthwise, remove seed and peel,
and immediately sprinkle with lemon juice to prevent discoloration
of the fruit. Fill each half with quartered strawberries, cubed peeled mango,
sliced peeled kiwi, plum wedges, and orange segments. Arrange
filled avocado halves on Belgian endive leaves.
Serve with any fruit dressing as desired.

Avocado Filled with Shrimp

Avocados may be filled with an assortment of foods, with shrimp
being a favorite filling. The photograph offers an avocado half filled
with cooked jumbo shrimps garnished with radicchio, curly endive,
pineapple segments, and baby corn.
A dressing of choice may accompany salad if desired.

Avocado Filled with Caviar

Yield: four servings

2 ripe large avocados, or 1 small honeydew, or medium cantaloupe

Lemon juice as needed

1 small head Belgian endive, cleaned and separated into leaves

About 4 ounces of caviar of choice

1 ripe medium tomato, cut into thin wedges, seeds and pulp removed

1 lemon, cut into thin wedges

Chopped peeled onion, chopped cooked egg white and egg yolk, sour cream, and toast points as desired for garnish

Cut avocados in half; remove peel and seed from each. Immediately sprinkle each with lemon juice to retard discoloration of the avocados. Cut a *very thin* slice from the rounded side of each half to form a base; turn each half cavity side up. Arrange endive leaves in the center of each avocado half. Spoon about 1 ounce of caviar over the endive leaves. Arrange tomato and lemon wedges alternately around each caviar serving. Serve each accompanied with chopped onion, chopped hard cooked egg white and egg yolk, sour cream, and toast points.

Bananas

The banana is a fruit which is eaten and enjoyed by many people; however, it is rarely used as a garnish because it browns quickly when it comes in contact with air. By brushing the peeled fruit with lemon or lime juice, the undesirable browning process can be eliminated.

Banana "Boats"

Watch young party-goers eyes dance when Banana "Boats" are served.
Combining imagination with edible delight, they may be served
alone or accompanied with ice cream and sauces.

Yield: one "boat"

1 firm ripe medium
 banana
Lemon juice as needed
1 orange or grapefruit
 section
Maraschino cherries as
 needed, drained
About 6 (4-inch)
 wooden skewers
About 1/4 cup prepared
 fruit of choice for
 garnish (seasonal
 berries, assorted
 melon balls, peach,
 pear, or nectarine
 slices, seedless
 grapes, pineapple
 cubes, or other
 desired fruit)
Fruit jelly of choice, as
 needed for glazing

To make the "boat", cut a thin slice from the outside curve of the banana to form a steady base, allowing the "boat" to stand upright. Peel back the top skin (from the inside curve) of the banana from tip, rolling back to the stem; secure rolled peel to "boat" with a short wooden pick (see photograph). Immediately brush exposed surface of the banana liberally with lemon juice to prevent browning of the fruit. Insert a 4-inch wooden skewer into the banana at end opposite rolled peel; attach an orange or grapefruit section to the top of the skewer to represent a "sail". Insert skewers into the sides of the banana extending outward, to represent "oars" used on a "Viking ship", about 2 to 3 per side. Attach a Maraschino cherry to end of each skewer to represent an "oar paddle". Garnish the "boat" with fruit and glaze with desired jelly.

Cantaloupe Filled with Sugared Lingonberries

*An excellent presentation for Thanksgiving or other holidays,
a cantaloupe filled with sugared lingonberries or cranberries
combines marvelous color and flavor accents with easy preparation.*

Yield: about eight servings

12 ounces thawed, frozen
  lingonberries or fresh
  cranberries
1 cup water
1 cup sugar
1 medium to large
  cantaloupe
Apple or cranberry jelly
  for glazing (optional)

In a deep medium heavy saucepan, combine berries, water, and sugar; cook over moderate heat, *just* until berries are ready to pop. Cool berries. Cut cantaloupe in half horizontally, using a zig-zag knife and design, if desired; scoop out pulp and seeds. Spoon sugared berries into cavities of melon halves and glaze with jelly, if desired. Arrange melon tureens on a service platter for presentation.

Figs

Figs are generally served as a dessert.
Often they are lightly sautéed in butter and accented
with Créme de Cassis. They also may be used as garnishes
or as part of a buffet presentation. In the photograph, fresh figs
have been cut in half and spiked with slivered blanched almonds
to represent the appearance of porcupines.
Thick slices, wedges, and cut star shapes of fruit top each.

Fruit Baskets and Fruit Displays

*D*isplaying fruit on platters or in baskets to attract the maximum of attention does not require much experience . . . but a good eye for detail, color and balance. For baskets, always choose four different colorful fruits.

*S*ome fruits might be shaped into stars or quarters to add more eye appeal to the platter. One fruit should act as the focal point of the arrangement.

Fruit on Mint Leaves with Strawberry Coulis

Yield: two servings

1 bunch mint leaves
1 medium to large banana
Lemon juice as needed
1 medium orange
1 small to medium grapefruit, red, pink, or white flesh as desired
About 4 to 5 strawberries for garnish, halved, leaves intact
About 6 strawberries for coulis
Curacao or Cointreau or other liqueur of choice, optional

Choose crisp mint leaves without blemishes; remove any grit from leaves, rinse, and gently pat dry with absorbent paper. Arrange mint leaves on a service plate. Peel and slice banana; immediately sprinkle with lemon juice to prevent discoloration of fruit. Arrange banana slices in a circular design over the mint leaves. Remove peel from orange and grapefruit; divide fruit into segments and arrange in the center of the banana slices, alternating orange and grapefruit sections. Garnish with strawberry halves. Place remaining strawberries in a blender container; cover and whiz until berries are puréed. Add liqueur as desired. Spoon mixture around outer rim of leaves.

Fruit and Vegetable "Wings"

*To obtain the best product for this garnish,
select fruits and/or vegetables with firm flesh and choose
a thin-blade knife for cutting. Using the following fruits
and vegetables results in the most interesting winged effect;
apples, pears, lemons, limes, oranges, tomatoes, radishes,
turnips,potatoes, and melons.*

Cut fruit or vegetable of choice in half. Use one half, cut surface turned up, as the base. Carefully make a "V" incision into the center part of the remaining fruit/vegetable half, bringing the two cuts together to separate the cut piece from the remaining fruit/vegetable. Repeat process two to three times more, being careful not to cut through the base (see illustration). Carefully separate each "V" piece to form a "wing". Sprinkle "V's" with lemon juice to prevent discoloration. Arrange "wings" as shown.

Sugared Grapes

Sugaring is a unique way of presenting grapes. Simple enough for the novice chef to prepare, these grapes are dramatic in appearance. They may be served as a large bunch from which guests may nibble. Or, they may be used in small clusters to enhance another food such as a roasted turkey.

Yield: about 10 to 12 small clusters

1 pound green, red, or black grapes, with seeds or seedless, as desired
1 cup sugar
2 egg whites, at room temperature
Sprigs of mint for garnish

Rinse grapes well and pat dry thoroughly with absorbent paper. With kitchen shears, cut grape bunch into small clusters. With a wire whisk or fork, whisk egg whites until foamy. With a pastry brush, paint grapes lightly with egg white, ensuring they are evenly coated. Place the grape clusters on a sheet of waxed paper; with a sieve or sifter, dust clusters with a thick coating of sugar. Repeat process as necessary. Allow grapes to stand at room temperature until coating is firm and dry. Arrange grapes as desired and garnish with sprigs of mint.

Artistic Kiwi Filled with Fruit Foam

*One of the most attractive fruits when sliced is the kiwi.
Although the outside is brown and covered with coarse hairy skin,
the inside is a bright green with a center of white and black rings.
Kiwi may be combined with other fruits to create a very colorful
fruit dish, or they may be used by themselves or as a garnish.*

Yield: four servings

Fruit Foam
4 firm ripe kiwi
  fruit
1 seedless orange,
  peeled and sliced
  crosswise, or
  sprigs of mint,
  or other berries
2 strawberries,
  cleaned, hulled,
  and quartered

Prepare Fruit Foam. Cut each kiwi fruit in half "Van Dyke-style" (zig-zag, see photograph). Fill each kiwi half with Fruit Foam, piling foam into a small mound. Garnish each with a strawberry quarter.

Note: Garnish with other foods as desired.

Fruit Foam

Yield: about one and one quarter cups

1/2 cup heavy
  cream, chilled
About 3 table -
  spoons puréed
  strawberries or
  other fruit (see
  note)
1 to 2 tablespoons
  sugar, or to taste

In a small bowl, beat cream at high speed of an electric mixer until stiff peaks are formed. Fold fruit purée and sugar into the whipped cream.

Note: To prepare purée, place a few strawberries in a blender container; cover and whiz at medium speed until fruit is puréed. Other fruit such as peaches, nectarines, pears, or berries may be used.

Lemon Garnishes

Lemons make a crisp and colorful garnish which can be used for a variety of dishes, fish being the most popular. They are also inexpensive and economical to use for large gatherings.

Lemon Slices and Twists

*These make an attractive as well as practical garnish
for hot and cold seafood or fish recipes.*

For each lemon, scrape the ink stamp from the yellow skin with the blunt end of a paring knife. Place the lemon in the left hand and grasp firmly around the center. (vice versa for the left handed person). Press the cutting blade of a canneller cutter into the skin at the top of the lemon, continuing to the bottom to form a line. Repeat procedure 5 times to form 6 uniform lines. Using a small sharp paring knife, cut the lemon into thin slices, about 1/16-inch thick. A lemon twist may be made by cutting the slice from the center to the edge, carefully twisting the "slit" onto a plate.

Lemon and Lime "Pigs"

*Simple to prepare, lemon and lime pigs are effective garnishes
to use as table decorations at children's parties.*

Yield: one "pig"

2 plump firm
  medium
  lemons
2 whole
  cloves, for
  "eyes"
1 medium
  lime
1/4 small
  cucumber
1 radish
4 short
  wooden
  picks

Carefully scrape off the ink stamp of one lemon. To make the "face", insert the cloves at the end of the lemon having a "snout". With a vegetable peeler, shave off a long piece of peel to use for the "ears", "tail" and "trotters" (legs). To make the "ears", carefully trim two small discs, equal in size, from the strip of peel. With a sharp knife, make two small incisions on the "face" end of the lemon, one at each side of "snout" and above and slightly to the side of the "eyes"; insert a disc into each cut. Turn lemon around, and having saved the length of peel, twist or tie it in a knot to create a "tail". Make an incision in the back end of the "pig" and insert the "tail" (see photograph) . Turn the "pig" upside down; cut a *very thin* slice from the underside to form a flat base so that when the "pig" is turned right side up, the "pig" rests on its "stomach" rather than its "legs". Cut 4 equal-size oval pieces about the length of a short wooden pick from the second lemon to use as "trotters". Make four incisions at equal points from each other in the underside of the "pig"; insert "trotters" into cuts, making sure that they extend out at

the side. Short wooden picks may be used in place of lemon pieces to simulate "trotters". To achieve an unusual effect, turn the "pig" upright and make four to five incisions across its back. Insert cucumber or radish slices into the cuts.

Lemon "Baskets" and "Stars"

Lemon "Baskets" make an excellent garnish for seafood recipes. They can be filled with any condiment or used just for eye appeal.

Yield: three "baskets"

3 lemons
Maraschino cherries, drained, as needed
1 large shrimp, cooked, peeled, and deveined
1 piece cooked langoustine (lobster), shell removed
Sprig of fresh dill weed

Prepare lemon "basket" and "stars" (see photograh). Fill the "basket" with langoustine and top with a Maraschino cherry. The "stars" may be garnished similarly with a shrimp and a sprig of dill weed or a Maraschino cherry.

Melon "Basket"

Any kind of melon, ie: cantaloupe, watermelon, crenshaw, honeydew,
casaba, Christmas, etc., may be used to prepare an elegant melon "basket".
An appealing and beautiful effect can be obtained by using
an assortment of melon balls with a variety of colors.

Yield: one "basket"

1 firm, *not too ripe*, medium to large melon of choice, blemish-free

2 cups melon balls, such as crenshaw, honeydew, watermelon, and cantaloupe balls

1/2 cup Curacao or other liqueur of choice

Mint sprig for garnish

It is important to cut the "handle" first. Place the melon on its side; with a sharp knife, cut half way down, slightly off center. Allow about a 1-inch wide "handle", then make a second cut to match the first cut. Cut horizontally around melon, about one third down from the top of the "handle", being careful not to cut through base of the "handle" (see photograph); carefully lift out the cut out portions. The shape of the "basket" should now be visible. Cut away the melon flesh under the "handle" with a small sharp knife; scoop out the remaining flesh in the base with a melon baller. In a deep medium bowl, combine melon balls and liqueur; cover and refrigerate until ready to serve, allowing melon balls to marinate in liqueur. Fill melon "basket" with melon balls and garnish with a mint sprig.

Melon Wedges or "Boats"

All kinds of melon may be garnished to create an interesting edible display.
Fresh mint leaves may be added to make a nice finishing touch.

Cut a melon into quarters lengthwise; large melons need to be cut into eighths. Cut or scoop the flesh out of the melon quarter or eighths, leaving shells. Cut the melon flesh into bite-size cubes or balls.

Fill watermelon shells with sliced, peeled bananas and top with melon balls. Or, fill each watermelon shell with a sliced peeled kiwi, mandarin orange sections, and slice peeled bananas.

Fill honeydew shell with melon balls and top with an orange slice cut into a "sail" shape and attached to the "boat" with a wooden pick. Accent the "sail" with a seedless red grape or sweet dark cherry. Or, cut cantaloupe or honeydew melons into quarters or eighths, forming boat shapes. With a sharp knife, slit the flesh from the shell/peel; leave the flesh in shell and cut into 1-inch thick segments. Extend melon segments outward slightly from the shell, alternating direction of segments to the left and right. Garnish each "boat" with an orange segment or peeled kiwi slice and a Maraschino or pitted sweet black cherry attached with a wooden pick.

Watermelon Filled with Fresh Fruit

Yield: eight to ten servings

1 large water-
melon
1 large orange
1 large banana
1 kiwi
1/2 large
pineapple
2 large apples,
divided
Lemon juice as
needed
Pineapple
leaves for
garnish

Cut the watermelon in half. Remove the flesh, cutting into cubes or balls; reserve for filling. Peel and cut orange, banana, kiwi, and pineapple into slices or bite-size pieces. Core and remove seeds from one apple, cut into bite-size pieces or thin slices. Sprinkle with lemon juice. Fill one watermelon shell half with the prepared fruits; discard second shell half. Thinly slice remaining apple; dip slices in lemon juice to prevent fruit from discoloration. Garnish watermelon with apple slices and pineapple leaves.

Melon Canapés

Melon canapés help to stimulate the palate and are especially appealing to those who are calorie and health conscious. Easy to prepare, these tidbits can be served at any large gathering including wedding receptions, cocktail parties, or graduation celebrations.

Yield: about 10 to 15 appetizer servings

1 large melon of choice for base (cantaloupe, watemelon, honeydew, crenshaw, etc.)
1 large honeydew
1 large cantaloupe
1 small watermelon
8 to 16 ounces prosciutto or Smithfield-style fully-cooked smoked ham, *very thinly sliced*
Frilled wooden picks

With a sharp knife or melon baller, cut or scoop flesh from all melons except the melon used as a base, into bite-size cubes or balls. Skewer each cube or ball with a frilled wooden pick and insert into the melon base (see photograph). Or, cut prosciutto or Smithfield-style ham slices into pieces large enough to fit around melon cubes or balls; wrap a piece of ham around each melon cube or ball and secure with a frilled wooden pick. Insert ham-wrapped melon pieces into melon base as previously directed.

Melon Easter "Rabbit"

*This sweet melon "rabbit" will be a hit at any party.
Although it is easy to prepare, one can be sure
that it will be the main attraction.*

Yield: one centerpiece

2 large honeydew
  melons or
  cantaloupe,
  for "body'
1 medium
  cantaloupe,
  for "ears"
1 large orange,
  for "hat"
15 to 20
  Maraschino
  cherries, for
  "necklace"
3 red grapes, for
  "eyes" and
  "nose"
Wooden picks
  and 2 (8-inch)
  skewers, for
  "arms"
2 cups green
  grapes,
  for "hands"
Flowered fabric
  napkin
  (optional)

With a sharp knife, cut a thin slice from the bottom of one honeydew melon or cantaloupe to allow it to stand upright. Arrange second melon (for "body") atop first melon; secure with wooden picks. Cut long cylindric ear shapes, keeping skin intact, from remaining melon (see photo- graph); place "ears" on top/"head" melon. Secure "ears" with wooden picks or by cutting small wedges into the "head". Secure the 3 grapes onto the front of the "head", two for "eyes", and one for the "nose", with wooden picks. Thread the two 8-inch skewers with green grapes to fashion "arms"; insert each into melon "body", one on either side. Secure orange as "hat" to "head" with wooden picks. Arrange the cherries around the "neck"/melon, securing each with a wooden pick

to the melon. Garnish "neck" with flowered fabric napkin (see photo- graph). Draw "whiskers" on melon "face" with a black marker. Gar- nish as desired.

Melon Pyramid

The Melon Pyramid is an easy to prepare edible centerpiece which adds dramatic interest to a buffet table. Later it may be taken apart and eaten.

Yield: two fruit centerpieces

1 large honeydew melon
1 medium cantaloupe
1 large apple
1 large lemon
1 kiwi
2 long wooden skewers
12 to 16 Maraschino cherries, drained
Short wooden picks as needed

With a sharp knife, cut melons and other fruits in half around their circumference in a large zig-zag pattern. Separate halves; remove seeds and pulp from melons. Stack the fruits (see photograph), starting with honeydew (largest) and ascending in order according to size, ending with the kiwi. Insert a long wooden skewer vertically through stacked fruits to secure well. Decorate the points of the honeydew melon with Maraschino cherries. Repeat process for second fruit pyramid.

Orange Garnishes

Oranges can be prepared in a variety of ways to create many different garnishes that are suitable for an assortment of occasions. Imaginative use with a zig-zag knife can produce star and crown shapes.

Orange or Lemon "Basket" Filled with Raspberries

Orange and Lemon "Baskets" make an attractive garnish for a wide variety
of food presentations and can be filled with many ingredients.
They offer an interesting alternative in which to serve
fruit or shrimp cocktail and make a striking accent for a cheeseboard.

Yield: one "basket"

1 medium
orange or
large lemon
5 fresh
raspberries
1 sprig of dill
weed or
mint
1 chive

With a sharp paring knife, cut a thin slice from the underside of the orange, allowing it to stand firmly upright. Cut a star shape (zig-zag pattern) around the orange, leaving a narrow strip to serve as the "handle" (see photograph). Cut away unwanted peel and orange segments, leaving an empty shell ("basket"); reserve discarded orange segments for orange salad or other use. Arrange dill weed sprig in "basket"; arrange raspberries over dill weed in "basket". Complete by wrapping and tying a chive around the center of the "handle" into a bow.

Orange "Boats" with Ham

*This is an attractive and fun garnish to create for children's parties.
It may also be used for any type of buffet.*

Yield: two "boats"

1 medium to large orange
2 thin fully-cooked smoked ham slices, about 3inches x 2-inches
2 thin cucumber slices, cut in the shape of a triangle
2 wooden picks, each about 2 inches in length

Carefully score orange with a sharp knife into quarters. Separate peel from the orange. Cut each ham slice into 2 equal pieces. Using one-quarter of peel as a "boat" base, roll ham half-slices jelly roll-style; place in "boat" base. Trim a second quarter to resemble a "sail"; thread a 2-inch wooden pick through 2 corners of the "sail." Insert into a ham roll. Finish off by attaching a triangle of cucumber to represent a "pennant" to the top of the pick, securing "sail". Repeat process for second "boat".

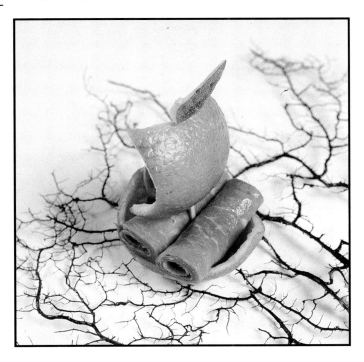

Woven "Baskets"

*Woven "Baskets" are easily prepared. Oranges, lemons, limes, or cucumbers
may be used to weave the basket. The rind or peel should be fairly strong
to withstand handling. Any fruit may be used as a filling. These "baskets"
may be used as a garnish for recipes prepared with prawns or crayfish,
or to serve with a fish entrée.*

Using a caneller cutter (see glossary of utensils) in a circular
motion, remove the peel of the fruit or cucumber in a long strand,
about 1/4 to 1/2-inch wide and as long as possible. Slice a second
fruit of choice or cucumber to create a base. Or, cut second fruit/
cucumber into a Van Dyke-shape. Rounds of toast may also be used
as a base. Insert wooden picks, about 1/2 to 3/4-inch apart, flaying
outward (see photograph). Starting at the base, weave the strand of
peel in and out around the wooden picks (see photo- graph).

Papaya Filled with Fruit

Yield: two servings

1 papaya
1 pint straw-
berries, hulled
and halved,
and/or
raspberries
Brandy or other
liqueur of
choice, as desired
Assorted fruits in
season, as
desired (peaches,
pears, kiwi,
nectarines,
bananas,
pineapple,
apples, etc.)
Mint sprigs
Pineapple leaves

With a sharp knife, cut papaya in half lengthwise; scoop out seeds and pulp from each half. Trim bottom of each half to allow papaya shells to rest firmly upright. Scoop out papaya flesh and cut into bite-size cubes. Peel and slice assorted seasonal fruits. Combine papaya with berries; spoon mixture into papaya shells, dividing evenly. Sprinkle each lightly with brandy or other liqueur, if desired. Arrange other fruits as illustrated. Garnish with sprigs of mint and pineapple leaves.

For an unusual treat, papaya can also be filled with delicious caviar.

Decorated Peaches

Peaches may be used in a variety of ways as garnishes. Poached fresh or canned peaches make excellent receptacles for many food fillings. The photographs illustrate some of the myriad of fillings available such as liver mousse with kiwi; cottage cheese, Maraschino cherry, and watercress; pyramid of olives or grapes; and chestnuts or chestnut purée.

Fresh Pear Halves Stuffed with Fruit or Seafood

This presentation is a very attractive way of serving fruit or seafood at the beginning of a meal, as well as on a cheese buffet. The following foods are merely suggestions . . . the actual possibilities are indefinite. The secret of this dish is to pick compatible fruits as the complement, taking into account size, flavor, and color. When garnishing a pear, always use small thin slices or quarters of fruit and have them overlap each other for eye appeal.

Yield: four servings

2 firm ripe pears as needed (Bartlett, Anjou, Comice, or Bosc)
1/2 cup water as needed
1/4 cup lemon juice as needed
1/8 teaspoon salt
Fruit filling, including strawberries, peeled seedless orange segments, sliced peeled kiwi, and/or sliced peeled peaches
Sprigs of mint for garnish
Shredded iceberg lettuce
Seafood Salad (optional) (see index)
1 hard cooked egg for garnish, peeled and grated

Use an unpeeled pear half cut lengthwise down the center of the pear, core and seeds removed, or a whole pear. Stand pear upright and remove a slice from the bulb end at an angle to form a base. On the opposite side of the bulb end, remove a larger slice of pear and scoop out fruit using a Parisian cutter (see glossary of cooking utensils). This will provide a cavity in which to place the fillings. Combine water, lemon juice, and salt; soak pears in mixture for several minutes to prevent discoloration. Drain pears well. Arrange prepared fruits of choice in pear cavities, overlapping each in an attractive design. Garnish each with fresh mint sprigs or line each pear cavity with shredded iceberg lettuce and then fill with prepared seafood filling. Garnish each with grated hard cooked egg or minced parsley. Serve the pears collectively arranged on a serving platter or on individual plates garnished with a bed of shredded iceberg lettuce and lemon and tomato wedges.

Note: The following guidelines are essential to ensure success in preparation of this recipe.
* *Always line the fruit shell with a lining of shredded lettuce or leaves to prevent the seafood from having a slightly sweet flavor.*
* *Always use small pieces of seafood that have been marinated in the dressing of choice.*

$\mathcal{P}ineapple\ "\mathcal{B}oat"\ of\ \mathcal{F}ruit\ \mathcal{S}alad$

Yield: ten to twelve servings

2 medium apples, cored, seeded, and cut into bite-size pieces

2 medium pears, cored, seeded, and cut into bite-size pieces

2 medium seedles oranges, peeled and sectioned

2 kiwi, peeled and sliced

1 peach, peeled and quartered

1 quart strawberries, cleaned, hulled, and quartered

Cointreau or other liqueur of choice, or orange or apple juice, as desired

1 large pineapple

10 to 12 raspberries for garnish

Mint sprigs for garnish

Prepare apples and pears; immediately sprinkle with lemon juice to prevent discoloration of fruit. In a deep bowl, combine apples, pears, oranges, kiwi, peach, and strawberries. Add liqueur of choice or orange or apple juice as desired to moisten salad and retain an appetizing look. Cover and refrigerate fruit salad until ready to serve. Choose a firm ripe pineapple with attractive green foliage. With a sharp knife, cut away vertically about one-fourth of the pineapple, leaving the leaves intact. Scoop or cut out pineapple flesh from fruit with leaves and cut away portions with a Parisienne scoop (see glossary of utensils) or spoon. Reserve shell with leaves attached for "boat". Cut flesh into bite-size cubes; add cubes to fruit salad, mixing lightly. Arrange pineapple shell on a service tray; spoon fruit salad into pineapple shell, allowing some to cascade over the sides. Garnish fruit "boat" with raspberries and mint sprigs.

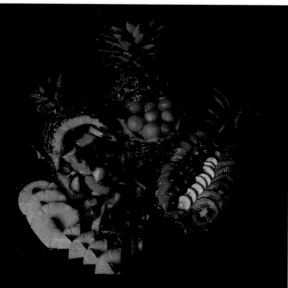

Pineapple with Fruit

Pineapple with Fruit is an attractive way to serve pineapple as an hors d'oeuvre or fruit plate. Any combination of fruits may be used together.

Yield: ten to twelve servings

1 large pineapple
1 small to medium honeydew melon, scooped out, seeds removed, and flesh formed into melon balls
1 medium cantaloupe, scooped out, seeds removed, and flesh formed into melon balls
1 large seedless orange, peeled and sliced
1 medium apple, peeled, cored, seeded, cut into thin slices, and sprinkled with lemon juice
Pitted sweet dark or Maraschino cherries, drained
6 to 8 seedless green or red grapes
A sprig of mint, for garnish

With a sharp knife, cut the pineapple horizontally into three equal sections. Decorate the top of the pineapple with melon balls as shown in the photograph. Scoop out the flesh from the bottom pineapple section to form a "bowl"; cut the removed flesh into bite-size pieces and return to the pineapple "bowl". Arrange pineapple sections as shown in photograph and decorate with orange and apple slices, melon balls, cherries, and grapes, or other choice of fruit. Garnish with a sprig of mint.

Sliced and Quartered Pineapple

Yield: four servings

1 firm ripe
  pineapple
1 medium seedless
  orange, peeled
  and divided into
  sections
  (optional)
1 plum, seeded
  and cut into
  wedges (optional)
A few raspberries
  (optional)
Trimmed
  pineapple leaves
  for garnish

With a sharp serrated knife, cut off top and bottom of pineapple. Carefully cut away the skin, retaining as much pineapple flesh as possible. Using a round pineapple cutter, cut down through the pineapple, removing the core. With a vegetable peeler, carefully remove any remaining pineapple "eyes" or skin. Cut pineapple into desired slices. Divide into four portions and garnish with orange sections, plum wedges, raspberries, or any combination of fruits and trimmed pineapple leaves and/or a sprig of mint.

Quartered Pineapple

Yield: four servings

1 firm ripe
  pineapple
Fruit as
  desired for
  garnish
Sprigs of mint

With a sharp serrated knife, cut pineapple in half lengthwise; cut each half lengthwise in half again. Carefully cut the flesh away from skin of each, keeping the flesh whole and leaving a shell. Cut the flesh into 1-inch segments and arrange in pineapple shells, dividing evenly. Slightly extend each pineapple segment outward from the shell, alternating each one in a right and left direction. Garnish each serving with fruit as desired and a sprig of mint.

Watermelon "Pirate Ship"

*This "pirate ship" may be done more elaborately depending upon the amount
of detail given to its design. For theme parties, assorted fresh fruits
may be placed in the ship for guests to nibble.*

Yield: one watermelon "pirate ship"

1 large water-
  melon, long
  shape and
  blemish-free
1 (15 to 20-inch)
  wooden skewer
  to secure "main
  sail"
2 (10 to 15-inch)
  wooden skewers
  to secure
  "support sails"
Short wooden
  picks, as needed

With a sharp 4-inch paring knife, cut a thin
slice horizontally from the base of the watermelon to allow it to stand upright. With a colored
pencil or a needle, mark the shape of the "pirate
ship" on the skin of the watermelon (see photograph). With a sharp knife, cut the melon horizontally along lines marked on melon, removing
about one-third of the melon. Reserve the top
rind of the melon for the "sails", cutting into 3
rectangles. Scoop out some of the melon flesh of
the base ("ship") portion of the melon with a
melon baller or spoon to give the "ship" more
character. From the reserved top portion, cut
small circles for "port holes"; fasten "port holes"
to the side of the "ship" with short wooden picks.
Insert long wooden skewers vertically into
reserved melon rind "sails"; then attach to top of
"boat" by inserting skewers into top of
"boat"/melon (see photograph).

Rudolf Sodamin

Meat
Poultry
Fish &
Seafood

Filet of Beef Bouquetiere

Yield: eight to ten servings

1 (3 to 4-pound)
  whole beef
  tenderloin
Glâce de Viande
  (see note)
Celery leaves,
  as needed
Turned vegetables
  including
  zucchini, carrots,
  and yellow
  summer squash
  (see index)
1 truffle, cut into
  thin slices and
  then cut
  into star
  shapes
  with a
  star-shaped
  cutter
  (optional)
  (see note)

Arrange tenderloin on a rack in a roasting pan. Insert a meat thermometer into the center of the tenderloin. Bake in a hot oven (400 degrees F.) for 20 to 25 minutes or until meat thermometer registers 130 to 140 degrees F. (medium rare). Allow tenderloin to stand for a few minutes at room temperature. With a sharp knife, cut tenderloin into 1-inch thick slices. Arrange tenderloin slices on a heated platter, overlapping slices. Garnish with celery leaves and Glâce de Viande. Serve with turned vegetables and truffle stars or vegetables of choice.

Note: Glâce de Viande is available in most supermarkets and specialty /gourmet grocery stores, or use brown beef sauce of choice.

Note: May use truffle paste (available in specialty/gourmet shops) in place of truffles if desired.

Cold Roast Rib of Beef

This is a stunning centerpiece for any cold buffet/meat presentation. Use imagination to create the desired decor. After the presentation, the roast may then be used in a cold beef salad to avoid any unnecessary waste.

Yield: one beef centerpiece

1 (8 to 10 pound) standing beef rib roast, including 4 rib bones
2 to 3 tablespoons hot cooking oil
2 cups Brown Sauce (see note)
About 2 cups Glazing Aspic (see index)
1 small bunch of broccoli
1 carrot, peeled, blanched (see glossary of cooking terms) and thinly sliced
4 plums, sliced and seeded
1 seedless orange, peeled and divided into sections
1 bunch parsley
Sprigs of fresh herbs as needed
Assorted sliced cold roasted meats (optional)

Prepare roast according to favorite recipe for standing beef rib roast. Cool. To dress the roast, remove from refrigerator, trim off all excess fat, sinew (gristle), and meat from the bony area of the roast. With a sharp knife, cut a thin slice of beef from each end of the roast, exposing the pink portion of the roast. Reserve discarded meat for a cold beef salad. Using a pastry brush, glaze the upper part of the roast nearest the bones with Brown Sauce. Chill in refrigerator to set glaze. Dip broccoli in aspic and arrange on the beef roast. In order, dip carrot slices, plum slices, and orange segments in aspic and arrange around broccoli on beef roast in an attractive design. Complete design with a border of parsley. Chill in refrigerator for at least 2 hours to allow garnish to set. Baste well with additional aspic and return to refrigerator to set. Repeat basting process once or twice more to create a more perfect looking finish.

Note: Canned Brown Sauce may be purchased in grocery and specialty food stores.

Garnished Turkey for a Buffet Table

The "Peacock" Turkey can be an effective complement to enhance a cold buffet.

1 (12 to 14-pound) turkey
About 5 to 6 cups mashed potatoes
20 medium tomatoes
About 1/2 cup Glazing Aspic, cooled almost to firming temperature (see index)
1/2 cup thin peeled carrot slices
1/4 to 1/2 cup pitted black olives
1/2 to 1 cup broccoli florets
1 black paper poster board, cut in the silhouette of a peacock head
2 large paper frills to garnish turkey legs (see index)
Crisp greens for garnish

Remove giblets and neck from body cavity. Rinse turkey and dry well. Fold neck skin behind turkey and fasten securely to the back with skewers. Lock wings behind the back (*akimbo*) and the drumsticks to the tail with heavy string. Place turkey on a rack in a roasting pan; brush entire bird lightly with oil. Cover loosely with aluminum foil, leaving openings at either end. Allow a hole for the meat thermometer and insert into the thickest part of the thigh muscle. Roast in a preheated slow oven (325 degrees F.) until done (about 20 to 25 minutes per pound); meat thermometer will register 180 degrees F. when the turkey is done. Remove foil about 45 minutes before end of cooking period to ensure even browning of bird. Cool and refrigerate for 12 hours.

To decorate turkey, carefully remove breasts from bird, leaving skin intact. Reserve cooked breast meat for other use. Fill cavities created in the turkey with mashed potatoes, recreating the prior appearance of the turkey. Carefully place turkey breast skin over mashed potato mounds. Blanch tomatoes in boiling water; drain, peel, and cut into wedges. Discard seeds, cover, dry between sheets of absorbent paper, and chill until ready to decorate the turkey. Starting at the top of the turkey, arrange the tomato wedges on the turkey to give the appearance of scales on a fish. Apply aspic to the turkey over the tomato wedges. (The cold turkey, as well as the cold tomato wedges, will allow the aspic to set and become firm immediately.) Return turkey to refrigerator to allow aspic to become fully set.

To create the peacock, arrange turkey breast, pointed downward, on a presentation board or platter. Arrange carrot slices, olives, and broccoli in a fan shape over turkey; attach "peacock head" silhouette, in the center of the fan at its base (see photograph). Baste "peacock" fan liberally with aspic; refrigerate until aspic becomes firm. Attach paper frills to turkey legs, pointing upward. Garnish base of turkey with crisp greens, or as desired.

"Flowering" Turkey

This presentation is a very attractive and unusual way of presenting a turkey for display, using a white Chaud Froid as the base and a selection of raw crisp vegetables to create the illusion of a cascading spray of flowers.

Stuffed Fillet of Sole
with Spinach Leaves and Lobster Mousse

An artistic way of presenting fish for a party,
stuffed fillet of sole may be prepared by experienced or novice chefs.

Yield: four servings

1 pound white fish fillet (sole, snapper, or turbot)
1 (1-pound) lobster (un-cooked)
4 eggs
1 cup heavy cream
3/4 cup (6-ounces) butter, at room temperature or melted
1 pound fresh spinach leaves, cleaned and stems removed
Salted boiling water, as needed
Wooden picks
Court Bouillon (see index

Clean the fish as necessary, removing skin and any bones. Using a sharp knife, flatten and trim the fish. The fish trimmings may be used as part of the mousse. Clean the lobster and cut meat into small pieces. In a bowl, combine lobster and fish trimmings; chill thoroughly. Place lobster-fish mixture in a food processor; add eggs, beating for about 5 minutes. Gradually add cream, being careful not to whip cream, as it might separate. Gradually add butter, a small amount at a time, until a smooth consistency is achieved and butter is completely incorporated into the mixture. Cover and chill mixture in refrigerator for about 3 hours.

In a large heavy saucepan, blanch spinach in boiling salted water to cover for 30 seconds; drain well and dry between sheets of absorbent paper. Using only the best looking leaves, arrange spinach leaves over fish fillet. Evenly spread lobster mousse over spinach making sure the mousse is not too thick. Roll fish fillet jelly roll-style; secure with wooden picks.

In a large heavy saucepan, poach fish roll in simmering Court Bouillon over moderate heat for 8 minutes. Or, cover fish roll in clear plastic wrap and arrange in a steamer on a rack over a small amount of simmering water. Cover and steam over moderate heat for 5 minutes. If poaching fish, allow to cool in it's own stock. Serve hot or chilled, as desired.

Oyster Platter

Yield: two servings

8 large *(count)* oysters, in shell

6 jumbo *(8 to 10 count)* shrimp, cooked, peeled, and deveined

Crushed ice, as needed

1 medium head Belgian endive

Crisp lettuce leaves, as desired

1 Lemon Star (see index)

Sprigs of dill weed for garnish

1 crayfish for garnish, cooked, whole and intact

1 small red, green, or yellow bell pepper, cored, seeded, and cut into cubes

American Cocktail Seafood Sauce (see index)

Choose *very fresh* oysters; scrub and open with an oyster knife. Leave oysters in the shell but loosen around the edges for easier eating. Arrange oysters and shrimp over a bed of crushed ice on a service plate. Garnish with Belgian endive leaves, lettuce leaves, sprigs of dill weed, and bell pepper cubes. Arrange Lemon "Star" and crayfish in the center of the platter. Accompany appetizer with American Cocktail Seafood Sauce.

Smoked Mussel and Shrimp Platter

Yield: two servings

6 large smoked mussels (see note)
6 jumbo *(16 to 20 count)* shrimp, cooked, peeled, deveined, and butterflied (see page 109)
1 bunch mustard or watercress
3 radishes, sliced
1 leek, cleaned and thinly sliced
1 medium carrot, peeled and cut into thin sticks
About 6 pitted black olives, cut into halves
Lime Vinegar Dressing, as desired (see index)

Prepare mussels and shrimp. Mussels may be arranged in mussel shells, if desired. Spread a bed of mustard or watercress over a large service plate. Arrange mussels and shrimp over cress. Garnish as desired with sliced radishes, sliced leek, carrot sticks, and olives. Serve with Lime Vinegar Dressing.

Note: Canned smoked mussels are available in grocery stores or specialty food/gourmet shops.

Shrimp Platter

Yield: six servings

2 pounds large (*21 to 35 count*) shrimp
4 crayfish for garnish
Simmering salted water, as needed
Curly endive (chicory)
1 head radicchio
1 bunch mustard or watercress
Sprigs of dill weed for garnish
American Cocktail Seafood Sauce (see index)

In a large heavy saucepan, cook shrimp and crayfish in about 3 quarts simmering salted water for about 3 to 5 minutes or until shells turn a coral pink. *Do not overcook.* Drain and rinse in cold water; drain again. Peel and devein shrimp; tails may be left intact, if desired. Chill until ready to use. Leave crayfish whole in shell; chill until ready to use. Clean curly endive and radicchio and drain well. Separate radicchio leaves and remove core. Dry thoroughly. Arrange radicchio, curly endive, and cress attractively on a serving platter. Arrange shrimp over bed of greens. Garnish with whole crayfish. Serve with American Cocktail Seafood Sauce.

Seafood "Flower"

*The Seafood "Flower" provides the pièce de résistance of snacks . . .
expensive but well worth the price and effort.*

Yield: two servings

5 cherry tomatoes
About 2 to 3
  teaspoons chopped
  peeled onion
About 5 teaspoons
  sour cream
About 5 teaspoons
  caviar of choice
6 jumbo *(16 to 20
  count)* shrimp,
  cooked, peeled,
  deveined, and
  tails intact
4 to 5 spinach
  leaves, cleaned,
  stems removed
1 small wedge red
  cabbage, cut in a
  julienne
1 small wedge
  green cabbage,
  cut in a julienne
1 ounce sharp
  Cheddar or
  American or Swiss
  or other cheese,
  cubed
1 ounce sharp
  Cheddar or
  American or Swiss
  or other cheese,
  grated
Sour Cream Onion
  Dressing, as
  desired (see index)

With a sharp knife, cut a *very thin* slice from the top of each cherry tomato. With a small melon scooper, carefully remove the insides of the tomatoes. Fill each tomato shell with about 1/2 teaspoon chopped onion, 1 teaspoon sour cream, and 1 teaspoon caviar. Arrange spinach leaves in an attractive flower design on a service plate. With a sharp knife, slit each shrimp lengthwise down the inside center of the shrimp, cutting each almost through (*butterflying*). Shrimp will open out flat but remain joined at the center. Arrange shrimp and stuffed tomatoes over outer area of spinach leaves. Arrange julienne of cabbage in a nest design in the center of the plate over the spinach leaves; fill "nest" with cubed and grated cheese. Serve with Sour Cream Onion Dressing.

CUNARD

In the Gracious presence of
HER MAJESTY THE QUEEN
AND
His Royal Highness
THE DUKE OF EDINBURGH
on the occasion of the Celebration of
the 150th Anniversary of The Cunard Line
FRIDAY 27TH JULY 1990

1840   1990

Gravlax "Butterflies" with Caviar

Elegant Gravlax "Butterflies" with Caviar is a distinctive presentation similar to one created for Her Majesty Queen Elizabeth II and Prince Phillip on the occasion of Cunard's one hundred fiftieth anniversary celebration on board the QE2.

Yield: four servings

1 pound salmon with skin, bones removed and cut into 2 fillets
2 tablespoons rock salt
2 tablespoons sugar
2 tablespoons white pepper
2 tablespoons black pepper
1 bunch dill weed (fresh only)
Crisp greens (optional)
4 tablespoons sour cream
4 tablespoons caviar
Chives for "antennae" garnish

Rinse salmon fillets and pat dry with absorbent paper. In a small bowl, combine salt, sugar, and peppers, mixing well. Rub mixture over all surfaces of salmon fillets. Arrange one fillet, skin side down, in a shallow glass or enamel baking dish; evenly spread half of the dill over the salmon in the dish. Top with remaining salmon fillet, skin side up. Spread remaining dill weed over second salmon fillet. Cover with plastic wrap or aluminum foil, securing tightly. Refrigerate for 4 days, turning salmon every 24 hours.

To serve, scrape off seasonings and pat salmon dry with absorbent paper. Place fillets, skin side down, on a wood cutting board. With a sharp, thin, flexible-blade knife, cut salmon into small pieces (see photograph). Arrange 6 salmon pieces similar to the wings of a butterfly (see photograph) on an appetizer plate lined with crisp greens, if desired. Fill a pastry/piping bag fitted with a nozzle, with sour cream; pipe about 1 tablespoon sour cream in a rounded rectangle shape in the center of the "butterfly". Spoon about 1 tablespoon caviar over the sour cream, allowing the sour cream to extend outward from the caviar (see photograph). Garnish the "butterfly" with 2 chives, each about 3 inches in length, representing the "antennaes". Repeat process three times more for a total of four "butterflies" or servings.

Salmon "Roses" with Caviar

This presentation is the classical Salmon a la Russe Deluxe.
It is a pièce de resistance of hors d'oeuvres.

Yield: eight "roses", four appetizer servings

24 thin slices smoked salmon, about 8 to 12 ounces total

About 4 ounces caviar of choice

Crisp salad greens (curly endive, radicchio, or Belgian endive)

Buttered toast points

Chopped hard cooked egg white

Grated hard cooked egg yolk

Chopped peeled onions

Sour cream or Horseradish Cream (see index)

For each "rose", overlap 3 salmon slices by approximately one-third the width of each slice; fold and roll the 3 slices into the shape of a "rose", opening the slices outward at one end of the roll in the manner of "flower petals" (see photograph). Repeat process for all "roses". Spoon about 1 teaspoon caviar into the center of each "rose".

Arrange three "roses" on each appetizer plate lined with crisp greens. Accompany each serving with buttered toast points, chopped hard cooked egg white, grated hard cooked egg yolk, chopped onions, and sour cream or Horseradish Cream.

Lobster Platter Facon du Chef Sodamin

Serve this lobster platter as a delicious, health conscious lunch.

Yield: four hors d'oeuvre or two entrée servings

1 (2 to 3-pound)
    lobster
2 pounds large
    spinach leaves
1 head Belgian
    endive
1 small head
    radicchio
1 lime or lemon,
    cut into a star
    shape (see index)
1 *very small* plum
    tomato
Yogurt Dill
    Sauce (see index)

In a large heavy kettle, bring salted water to a boil over high heat. Plunge lobster into boiling water, head first. Reduce heat, cover, and simmer for 8 to 10 minutes, or until lobster turns red. Drain and crack shell, and remove meat when lobster is cool enough to handle.

Clean spinach, endive, and radicchio, removing all sand and grit; separate leaves, drain well, and pat dry between sheets of absorbent paper. Arrange spinach leaves as a base on a platter. Arrange endive leaves, then radicchio leaves over spinach. With a sharp knife, cut cooked lobster in shell in half, lengthwise.

Arrange lobster halves over spinach bed, each at opposite ends of platter, facing, or tail to tail. Arrange legs as shown in photograph, equal distance apart. Place cherry tomato in center of lime star and then place in the center of the platter. Serve with Yogurt Dill Sauce or other dressing of choice.

Seafood Salad

Yield: four servings

4 jumbo (*8 to 10 count*) shrimp
2 ounces very small (*50 to 60 count*) shrimp
4 scallops (sea or bay)
2 ounces whitefish (sea trout, sole, flounder, or other delicate-flavored white-fleshed fish)
Dijon Vinaigrette Dressing
1 (6 1/2-ounce) can squid, drained, and cut into rings
12 spinach leaves
4 crisp radicchio leaves
4 sprigs curly endive (chicory)

In a medium heavy saucepan, cook *all* shrimp in about 1 to 1 1/2 quarts simmering salted water for 3 to 5 minutes. *Do not overcook.* Immediately rinse in cold water; drain well. Remove peel, tails, and devein. Reserve jumbo shrimp for garnish. In a medium heavy saucepan, poach scallops and white-fleshed fish in simmering fish stock or wine until done, about 3 to 5 minutes, for scallops and about 4 to 5 minutes for fish; drain, rinse in cold running water, and drain well again. *Do not overcook* scallops, as they will become tough. Cut fish into bite-size pieces. Prepare dressing. When seafood is thoroughly cool, combine with dressing and add squid, tossing lightly to mix. Arrange 3 spinach leaves, a radicchio leaf, and a sprig of curly endive on each luncheon plate. Spoon seafood salad into the center of the salad greens, dividing evenly. Garnish as desired.

Dijon Vinaigrette Dressing

Yield: about one and one quarter cups

2 tablespoons balsamic vinegar
1 teaspoon Dijon-style prepared mustard
1 cup salad oil
1 garlic clove, peeled and minced
1 teaspoon minced parsley
1 teaspoon minced peeled onion
Salt and white pepper to taste (optional)

In a small bowl, combine vinegar and mustard, blending well. With a wire whisk, gradually beat in oil, whisking until mixture is smooth and thick. Stir in garlic, parsley, and onion. Season with salt and pepper to taste, if desired.

Rudolf Sodamin

Cheese and Egg Garnishes & Recipes

Cheese, Fruit, and Vegetable "Basket"

An attractive and exciting way to serve cheese is in a bread "gondola" accented with vegetable sticks, fruit pieces, bell pepper and cucumber slices, cherry tomatoes, and olives. The choice of a "basket" may vary in color, style, and content. . .according to the artistic dictates of the chef.

Cream Cheese "Mushrooms"

Cheese is an interesting option to use for the preparation of healthy canapés or hors d'oeuvres. There are many varieties, sizes, colors, and shapes available. With cheese one can allow the imagination to expand in developing artistic food creations. Cheeseboards are mostly served with fruit and vegetables, i.e., grapes, pears, bell pepper slices, radishes or even with nuts and salted bread sticks. It is also an excellent accompaniment for wines.

Yield: about 12 medium "mushrooms"

1 (8- ounce) package cream cheese, at room temperature
1 tablespoon paprika, as needed

With the hands, work the cream cheese for a few minutes to soften sufficiently. *Do not overwork* cheese or it will be difficult to handle. To form a "stem", mold a small amount of cream cheese into a triangular, mushroom shape. To form a "mushroom cap", roll a small amount of cheese into a ball; press the center of the ball lightly to flatten as a "mushroom cap" looks. Sprinkle top of "mushroom cap" liberally with paprika. Place "mushroom cap" on top of "stem". Repeat process until all cream cheese is used. With a sharp small knife, cut away very small circles in paprika "mushroom caps" to give effect of spots (see photograph).

Versatile Cheese Board

*A cheese board display of a variety of cheeses
allows creativity to reign. Cheese of different shapes
should be arranged diagonally. The illustrated arrangement
includes smoked Cheddar, Edam, Boursin, Roquefurt, smoked Gouda,
Camembert, and Swiss cheeses accented with radishes, watercress,
bell peppers, cherry tomatoes, egg "mushrooms", and
an orange half filled with grapes.*

Cheese Canapés on Edam's "Face"

Yield: fourteen appetizer servings

Mayonnaise, butter, or
  margarine, at room
  temperature
Crisp lettuce leaves
1 round Edam cheese,
  about 8 to 16 ounces
7 ounces Swiss cheese, cut
  into 1/2 to 3/4-inch cubes
7 ounces Camembert, cut
  into bite-size pieces
7 ounces blue cheese, cut
  into bite-size pieces
7 ounces Mozzarella
  cheese, formed into
  balls or 1/2 to 3/4-inch
  cubes
Minced Parsley
Cherry Tomatoes
About 30 seedless red or
  green grapes
About 30 pimento-stuffed
  medium green olives or
  pitted black olives,
  drained
Frilled short wooden
  picks, as needed

Evenly spread bread slices with mayonnaise or butter. Top each with a lettuce leaf. Cut each with a small biscuit cutter (1 1/2-inches in diameter) or sharp knife into circles or triangles. Arrange the various flavored cheese cubes on the bread circles and triangles. Top each with a grape or an olive. Skewer each with a frilled wooden pick to Edam cheese "face". To serve, arrange on a service plate.

Cheese Grape "Girl"

A charming centerpiece presentation for children
and teenage parties, the Cheese Grape "Girl" is also an ideal accent
for cheese platters and decoration for a buffet. It also provides
an interesting conversation piece for wine and cheese parties.

Yield: one centerpiece

2 medium Edam
  cheeses, each
  about 2 pounds
  (approximately
  the size of a large
  grapefruit, about 6-
  inches in diameter)
1 (4 to 5-inch)
  wooden skewer
8 ounces seedless
  red grapes
2 round paper
  doilies (about 8-
  inches in diameter)
Short wooden picks,
  as needed
1 bunch parsley or
1 pound broccoli,
  cut into florets
1 small fabric bow
  (optional)

To make the Cheese Grape "Girl", cut a thin slice from one side of each cheese. Place paper doilies between the cheeses, flat side to round top. Fasten cheeses together, flat side of one to round side of second cheese vertically through the center of the cheeses with a long wooden skewer. With a sharp 3 to 4-inch knife, cut away design for the "face" from the top cheese by removing the red rind (see photograph). Repeat process on the second cheese for the "body" design.

Remove grapes from stems and stalk; insert a short wooden pick into each grape and then fasten to the cheese/"head" with the opposite end of the pick (see photograph). Arrange cheese "girl" on a serving platter or board, then arrange large sprigs of parsley or large broccoli florets around the base of the cheese "girl" to simulate a skirt. Attach bow to grape "coiffure" with a wooden pick inserted into the top cheese.

Cheese "Mice"

*Cheese "Mice" suggest a playful garnish. It is one that allows
the personal creativity of a cook to shine. In addition to
the ingredients, a sharp knife and a dash of childishness is needed.*

Yield: about five to six "mice"

2 (1 1/2 to 3-
 pound) blocks of
 hard cheese,such
 as Swiss or white
 Cheddar
2 to 3 radishes
Wooden picks,
 as needed
15 to 18 whole
 cloves, black
 peppercorns,
 slivers of chives,
 or pitted black
 olives, for eyes
 and nose
5 to 6 radish roots

With a sharp knife, cut one cheese block into oblong/rectangular shapes of desired size. Carve the top of each oblong into a rounded sloping egg shape, ending in a point that will become the "nose". Cut thin slivers from the radishes to form "ears"; for larger "mice", shape small pieces of cheese for "ears". Attach "ears" to head end of each "mouse" with wooden picks. Use whole cloves, peppercorns, slivers of chives, or black olives as "eyes" and "nose" for each "mouse" (see photograph). Arrange "mice" atop second block of cheese to display.

Eggs

With the creamy white color of the egg white and bright yellow of the yolk, the contrasting colors and textures in eggs blend perfectly with many other food products to create visually interesting and appetizing accompaniments. Fantasy may be incorporated into many egg garnishes at the cook's discretion.

Egg Mousse

Yield: six egg halves

3 jumbo or extra large eggs, at room temperature
1/2 cup butter or margarine, at room temperature
Salt and white pepper to taste

Using a sharp knife, cut each egg in half lengthwise. Wet the blade first to ensure the cut being clear and clean. Cut a *very, very thin* slice from the rounded part of each half to allow the egg to stand upright easily. Carefully scoop out the yolks from the whites. In a small deep bowl, mash the yolks thoroughly. Add butter and beat until mixture is smooth and creamy. Season with salt and pepper to taste. Using a pastry/piping bag fitted with a star nozzle, fill bag with egg mixture; pipe a rosette into each egg white shell. Serve as is, or further decorate eggs as desired.

EGGS MORNAY: Using the previously prepared egg mousse (yolk mixture), add about 2 tablespoons room temperature butter or margarine; mix until mixture is firm. As shown in the photograph (starting at the top and going clockwise) the following accompaniments may be added. Using an egg white half filled with egg yolk mousse, place 2 cherry tomato crowns, one inside of the other in the center of the mousse. Garnish with a sprig of dill weed or parsley.

Stuffed Deviled Eggs

Starting at the top of the photograph and working clockwise.

* Using one of the stuffed eggs, place a pimento stuffed olive crown in the center of the yolk rosette. Working away from the crown toward the tip of egg white, place slices of black and green olive in "V" shape arrangements.
* Using one of the unstuffed cut egg halves, place half slices of pimento stuffed olives around the egg half. Arrange six triangular shaped pieces of black olive in a star shape in the center of the egg, leaving enough space in the middle for a small dollop of mayonnaise or sour cream. Top with a small tomato "diamond".
* Using one of the stuffed egg halves, place three triangular slices of black olive at the base of the egg facing the tip of the egg. Place thin slice of tomato into the contours of the piped egg yolk mixture. Garnish with a small sprig of parsley.
* Place an olive crown in the center of one of the unstuffed egg halves. Surround with sliced tomato triangles to form a seven pointed star. Place a slice of olive between each point.
* For a simple but effective egg garnish, place an olive crown in the center of a half crowned egg.

Egg and Tomato Garnishes

Clown

Yield: one garnish

1 hard cooked
egg, shell
removed
1 (1/2-inch) thick
slice cucumber
Mayonnaise, as
desired
Yellow and red
food coloring
(optional)
2 whole cloves
1 thin slice of
pimento-
stuffed green
olive

With a sharp knife, cut a *very thin* slice from the bottom of the egg so that it will stand firmly erect. Place egg, rounded side up, on cucumber slice. Fill a pastry/piping bag fitted with a nozzle with mayonnaise; pipe around the top of the egg to simulate hair (mayonnaise may be tinted yellow or red-orange with edible food coloring, if desired). Place the cloves on the egg to form "eyes" and attach the olive slice and piece of cucumber skin to form a "nose" and "mouth" (see photograph).

Egg "Frog Princess" on Cabbage

Yield: four "frogs" on a "lily pad"

4 hard cooked eggs, peeled
Short wooden picks, as needed
1 cup White Chaud Froid Sauce, for glazing the eggs (see index)
1/4 cup minced blanched spinach
Cucumber skin, cut into 8 circles, each 1/4-inch in diameter, for "eyes"
Red bell pepper skin, cut into 8 small thin strips to shape for "mouths"
1 carrot, peeled and blanched, cut into 1-inch cubes
2 cabbage leaves, 1 whole and 1 shredded

With a sharp knife, cut slice from one side of each egg so that the eggs stand firmly on a diagonal or a slant. The slice of egg which has been cut away is used to form the "legs" of each "frog". Fasten each "leg" with a wooden pick. In a small bowl, combine Chaud Froid with spinach, mixing well. With a pastry brush, coat the top of each egg/"frog" thoroughly with sauce to simulate hair. To form "eyes", carefully place 2 cucumber skin circles on each egg. Arrange 2 small strips of red bell pepper in a small circle to form "mouth" (see photograph). Attach carrot "cubes" to top of eggs, securing with wooden picks (see photograph). Carefully arrange "frogs" on a serving plate lined with a whole cabbage leaf. Arrange shredded cabbage around "lily pad". Chill until ready to display.

Egg Chickens and Frogs

Egg Mousse (see index) is piped onto peeled hard cooked eggs, forming the "heads", "wings", and "tails" of the "chickens". The garnish is completed with slivers of red bell pepper used for the "eyes" and "beak". Parsley represents the comb. A quail egg may also be used for the "head". For the "frogs", very thin slices are cut from some of the eggs to secure bases. "Feet" and "faces" are formed with carrot pieces.

Poached Egg Platter

Yield: two servings

4 large eggs
4 slices cucumber or whole wheat toast points
Charon Sauce
2 tablespoons minced chives
1/2 small green or red bell pepper, cut in julienne-style
Sprigs of dill weed and mustard or watercress for garnish

In a deep heavy skillet, poach eggs in simmering water for about 3 to 4 minutes or until egg yolks are of desired consistency. Remove eggs from water, being careful not to break eggs. Arrange two eggs over cucumber slices or toast points on individual plates. Or, arrange all eggs over cucumber slices or toast points on a service platter. Top each egg with a tablespoon of Charon Sauce and garnish with julienne of bell pepper and sprigs of dill weed and mustard or watercress.

Charon Sauce

Yield: about one half cup

2 egg yolks
1 tablespoon warm water
1 teaspoon tarragon vinegar
6 tablespoons clarified butter, (see note)
1 tablespoon ketchup
1 teaspoon tomato paste
4 to 5 drops Worcestershire sauce
Salt and pepper to taste

Place the egg yolks in the top of a double boiler; add water and tarragon vinegar. With a wire whisk, vigorously whisk egg yolks over *hot, not boiling*, water until egg yolks become a thick foamy consistency. *Be careful not to cook the egg yolks.* Slowly whisk in the melted, clarified butter, until it is all blended into the egg yolks. Fold in ketchup and tomato paste. Add Worcestershire sauce and salt and pepper to taste.

Note: To prepare clarified butter, melt butter in a small heavy saucepan over low heat. Pour melted butter into a small bowl and allow to cool at room temperature. Skim off the pure fat collecting at the top of the bowl and discard the remaining solids and water.

Rudolf Sodamin

Assorted Garnishes & Recipes

"Rose" Garnishes

"Rose" garnishes are a very effective and colorful way to garnish or decorate food, as well as making a centerpiece. "Roses" are made from fruits and vegetables. The first "rose" may not be perfect, but a little practice makes perfect. The accompanying photograph shows various "roses" on a plate surrounded by symmetrically sliced vegetables. For this decoration to be most effective, positioning of color and size of the "roses" must harmonize. One of the most popular foods from which to make "roses" is the tomato. The illustration shows how the skin is peeled very thinly. Use a sharp new vegetable peeler or a sharp small knife for the best results.

Fruits or vegetables to use to make "roses" include:

Apples, red or green
Apricots, yellow
Grapefruit, yellow or pink
Lemons, yellow
Limes, bright green
Oranges, orange
Nectarines, red or yellow
Plums, dark red or purple
Tomatoes, red or green

Using a sharp, small paring knife and taking the tomato in one hand, horizontally slice across three-fourths of the way through the top, leaving it connected to the whole tomato. Slowly and evenly peel the tomato, keeping the skin intact. When the tomato is completely peeled, roll the end of the peel which was cut last between the forefinger and thumb, keeping it fairly taut. The top of the tomato which was sliced away first will become the base of the "rose" (see illustration). The color of the "rose" may be intensified by placing a darker color accent underneath the "rose". Use fresh basil or mint leaves or a sprig of fresh dill weed as accents.

Jellied Aspic in Fruit

*Jellied Aspic in Fruit is an interesting but simple fruit decoration
which can be used for buffets or sit-down dinners. There are several
different flavors of gelatin available which look very effective served
in wedges or slices of fruit. Cranberry or mint jelly may also be served
in the same manner with the addition of unflavored gelatin to the hot mixture.*

Yield: six to eight servings

1 honeydew melon
or cantaloupe
3 to 4 large oranges
or 4 to 6 large
lemons
1 (3-ounce) package
gelatin, flavor of
choice

Choose a large piece of fruit such as a honeydew melon or cantaloupe. With a sharp knife, cut in half crosswise. Remove pulp and seeds. Be careful not to create a hole in the fruit. Place melon half on the inside of an egg carton or a muffin baking pan to ensure melon standing upright. Oranges or lemons may also be used in place of melons. Remove seeds and pulp, leaving shell.

Prepare gelatin according to package directions; cool to room temperature and pour into melon, orange, or lemon halves. Carefully transfer fruit filled with gelatin to refrigerator; chill at least 2 hours until gelatin is firm. Heat a sharp knife blade in hot water; thoroughly dry. Slice fruit into wedges or slices as desired. A serrated or zig-zag knife may be used to achieve a different texture.

Note: Do not use kiwi, papaya, mango, or fresh pineapple as these fruits contain enzymes which will prevent the gelatin from setting or becoming firm.

Aspic

*Aspic, also known as jelly, is mostly used for chemising (glazing) dishes
to keep them fresh. The aspic must be allowed to set (begins to thicken)
as long as possible before using; however, it should be used while
it is still lukewarm and runny. It should not be stirred too much
as stirring creates air bubbles.*

Assorted Canapés

Herring Canapés

Yield: one canapé per piece of herring

Place a bite-size piece of marinated herring on a slice of cold peeled boiled potato and garnish with a dollop of sour cream and a thin ring of leek. Repeat process for as many canapés as desired.

Seafood Salad on Artichoke Leaf

Yield: one canapé per artichoke leaf

Spoon a small amount of Seafood Salad (see index) on the edible portion of a cooked artichoke leaf. Repeat process for as many canapés as desired. Use drained canned artichoke leaves, or frozen artichoke leaves, cooked according to package directions, or cooked fresh artichokes (see index). Minced cooked chicken, cooked, peeled shrimp, or flaked crabmeat may be used plain or made into a salad.

Cucumber "Basket" Filled with Shrimp

Yield: six to eight canapés per cucumber

Cut a medium cucumber into 1 1/2-inch segments. Scoop each segment out to form a shell. Fill each with marinated, peeled, cooked, *very small* shrimp pieces or crabmeat salad and garnish with a sprig of dill weed. Repeat process for as many canapés as desired.

Photo top left: Cheese canapés.
Photo right: Spoon canapés.

Kenneth's Giant Sandwich

*This whimsical looking sandwich is guaranteed to be the center
of attention at any children's party.
Any filling desirable to a kid's appetite may be used.*

Yield: six servings

1 long baquette
French bread,
about 1 pound
Mayonnaise as
desired (about 1
cup)
Crisp lettuce leaves
as desired
2 thin slices sharp
Cheddar, Ameri-
can, Swiss, or
other cheese
2 thin slices fully-
cooked smoked
ham
1 hard cooked egg,
peeled and sliced
1 small cucumber
1 small tomato,
thinly sliced
2 to 3 radishes, thin-
ly sliced
1 small onion, peel-
ed and thinly
sliced
2 pitted black olives
for "eyes"
Sliver of red bell
pepper for
"tongue"

With a sharp serrated knife, cut the bread in half lengthwise; then cut each half into six equal segments. Lightly spread cut surfaces of bread with mayonnaise. Arrange crisp lettuce leaves on one half of the bread sections. Arrange cheese, ham, or egg slices over lettuce topped bread sections. Cut a small piece of the skin from the cucumber in a zig-zag strip to represent "teeth" and two small triangles for "eyes"; thinly slice the remaining portion of the cucumber for the sandwich. Top each sandwich with cucumber, tomato, radish and/or onion slices. Each segment of the sandwich should have a different filling. Other fillings of choice may be used as desired. Top each sandwich segment with a second segment of bread. Arrange sandwich segments on a service plate as shown in photograph. Arrange zig-zag strip of cucumber on the first sandwich segment to represent "teeth"; add pepper strips to represent "tongue". Place the cucumber triangles and olives above the "teeth" to represent the "nose" and "eyes". Fill a pastry/piping bag, fitted with a nozzle, with mayonnaise; pipe mayonnaise at the top of each segment for the "fins" and garnish each with cucumber slices.

Paper Frills for Poultry and Lamb Chops

Yield: frill for one poultry drumstick or lamb chop

1 sheet rectangular paper, white or any desired color, about 3 x 2 1/2 inches
1 pair scissors
Clear sticky tape for fastening as needed, or staples

Fold paper in half lengthwise. Do not crease fold. With scissors, cut at right angles to the folded edge, with cuts approximately 1/2 inch in length, about 1/8 inch apart, to the end of the paper (see illustration). The closer the cuts are made to each other, the more "frilly" will be the effect. Roll the paper around a poultry drumstick bone or lamb chop bone; secure frill tightly with tape.

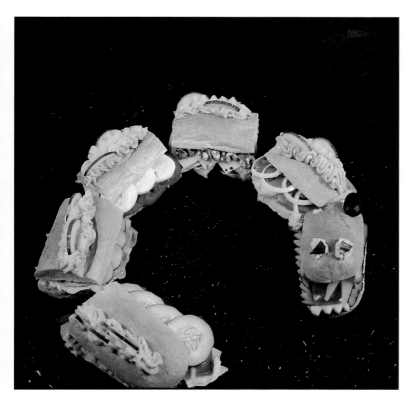

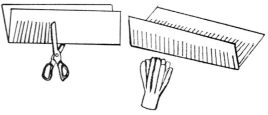

Chicken Mousse

Yield: four servings

4 slices white bread
1/4 cup milk
4 chicken breasts,
  skinned and boned
Pinch of nutmeg
Salt and pepper to taste

In a small bowl, soak bread in milk until all liquid is absorbed to form a *panade*. Cut chicken breasts into pieces. Place chicken in a blender container; add panade. Cover and whiz at medium speed until mixture is puréed. Pour into 4 buttered individual soufflé dishes, dividing evenly (see baking note).

Vegetable Mousse

Yield: four servings

4 eggs
2 cups, plus 1 tablespoon milk
1 cup cooked vegetable purée (see note)
1/2 teaspoon salt
1/2 teaspoon nutmeg
1/2 teaspoon white pepper

In a medium bowl, with a wire whisk, beat eggs, one at a time, into the milk. Add puréed vegetable and seasonings, blending well. Pour mixture into 4 buttered individual soufflé dishes, dividing evenly.
Note: Cook vegetables to be puréed until just tender. Do not overcook (see baking note).

Seafood Mousse

Yield: four servings

4 asparagus spears
4 ounces whitefish, flounder, salmon, ocean trout, or other delicate-flavored whitefish), skinned and minced
1 egg white
1 1/2 tablespoons lemon juice
Pinch of cayenne pepper
Pinch of white pepper
6 tablespoons light cream, or half-and-half
2 envelopes (tablespoons) unflavored gelatin
3 to 4 tablespoons warm water
Butter or margarine as needed, at room temperature
Minted Yogurt Dressing
1 medium tomato, chopped, seeds discarded
4 sprigs of mint for garnish
About 4 teaspoons grated lemon peel

Prepare asparagus, and remove woody portion. Cut the stalks into 1/2-inch pieces, reserving about 1 to 1 1/2 inches for the tips. In a small heavy saucepan, cook tips and pieces in boiling salted water until tender but crisp, about 8 minutes; drain well and refresh immediately in ice water. Reserve for mousse and garnish.

Place minced fish in a medium bowl; cover and refrigerate for two hours. Place fish in bowl in a larger bowl filled with a bed of crushed ice or ice cubes. Add egg white, lemon juice, and peppers, beating well at high speed of an electric mixer. Gradually beat in cream, a little at a time. In a 1-cup measure, soften gelatin in warm water; stir into mousse mixture, mixing well. Fold asparagus pieces into mousse.

Lightly butter 4 (3-ounce) soufflé or timbale dishes; spoon mousse into each, dividing evenly (see baking note).

To serve hot, loosen mousse from soufflé dishes and turn out onto individual plates. To serve chilled mousse, spoon about 2 tablespoons of Minted Yogurt Dressing onto each of 4 luncheon plates. Garnish each serving with chopped tomato, a sprig of mint, and about 1 teaspoon grated lemon peel.

Note: Arrange filled soufflé dishes in a 9x9x2-inch baking dish; add enough hot water to fill baking dish halfway with water. Cover mousse with aluminum foil and bake in a moderate oven (350 degrees F.) for 20 to 25 minutes or until soufflés are set.

Chicken Liver Mousse

Yield: four servings

1 pound chicken livers
1/3 cup chopped peeled
   onion
1/2 tablespoon minced
   fresh majoram
6 tablespoons butter or
   margarine, melted
3 to 4 tablespoons brandy
2 eggs plus 1 egg yolk
3/4 cup heavy cream,
   divided
Salt and pepper to taste

In a medium heavy skillet, sauté chicken livers and onion in butter over moderate heat until livers are browned on the outside and light pink on the inside, and onions are tender but not browned. *Do not overcook.* Sprinkle brandy over mixture; transfer to a blender container. Add eggs and yolk and half the cream; cover and whiz until mixture is puréed. Place in refrigerator until mixture is thoroughly chilled. Chill remaining cream and then beat in a chilled bowl with chilled beaters until soft peaks are formed. Fold whip-ped cream into chilled chicken liver mixture. Season with salt and pepper to taste. Pour mixture into 4 buttered individual soufflé dishes, dividing evenly (see baking note page 138).

Lime Vinegar Dressing

Yield: about two cups

10 shallots
2 garlic cloves
1 teaspoon minced
   pimentos, drained
1/2 teaspoon chopped
   chives, or green (spring)
   onions
1/2 teaspoon chopped
   parsley
10 limes
1/4 cup white vinegar
2 teaspoons sugar
1 teaspoon Dijon-style
   prepared mustard
1 cup olive oil
1/2 teaspoon freshly
   ground black pepper-
   corns
Salt to taste

Peel shallots and garlic cloves, finely chop, and place in a small bowl. Add pimentos, chives or green onions, and parsley, mixing lightly. Extract juice from limes and place in a small bowl. Add vinegar, sugar, and mustard, blending well. With a wire whisk, gradually add olive oil, beating well until mixture is thickened; stir into shallot mixture. Add pepper and salt to taste, mixing well. Chill for two hours to blend flavors.

Sour Cream Onion Dressing

Yield: about three cups

1 1/2 cups sour cream or
   unflavored yogurt
1 cup light cream
3 tablespoons minced
   peeled onion
1/2 cup minced parsley
Salt and pepper to taste

In a small bowl, combine the first 4 ingredients. Add salt and pepper to taste, blending well.

Minted Yogurt Dressing

Yield: about one half cup

1/4 cup unflavored
   yogurt
2 sprigs of mint, minced

1 1/2 tablespoons lemon
   juice
Pinch of white pepper, or
   to taste
Water as needed

In a small bowl, combine all ingredients, whisking well to mix. If dressing is too thick, blend in a few drops of water to achieve desired consistency.

Yogurt Dill Sauce

Yield: two and three fourths cups

1 cup unflavored yogurt
   (regular or low-fat)
1 cup sour cream
1/2 cup light cream or
   half-and-half
About 2 to 3 tablespoons
   minced dill weed leaves
Salt and pepper to taste

In a small bowl, combine yogurt and sour cream, blending well. Gradually add cream, blending to desired consistency. Add dill weed and salt and pepper to taste, blending well.

Rudolf Sodamin

American Cocktail Seafood Sauce

Yield: About two and three fourths cups

1 cup ketchup
1 cup chili sauce
1/2 cup orange juice
2 tablespoons Cognac or brandy
2 tablespoons bottled prepared grated horseradish
1 teaspoon Worcestershire sauce
10 drops Tabasco sauce
Pinch of sugar
Pepper to taste

In a small bowl, combine ketchup, chili sauce, orange juice, Cognac, prepared horseradish, Worcestershire and Tabasco sauces, blending well. Add sugar and pepper to taste. Cover and refrigerate for at least 2 hours to allow flavors to blend.

Note: To increase the spiciness of the sauce, add more prepared horseradish and Tabasco sauce to taste.

White Chaud Froid Sauce

Yield: six cups

5 pounds meaty veal bones, including shanks and skin
6 carrots, peeled and coarsely chopped
2 parsnips, peeled and coarsley chopped
2 onions, peeled and coarsely chopped
1 celery rib, coarsely chopped
Water as needed
2 garlic cloves, peeled and coarsely chopped
2 cups dry white wine
6 tablespoons lemon juice
Salt and pepper to taste
4 cups heavy cream
2 egg yolks, lightly beaten
Unflavored gelatin as needed (optional)

Cut bones as small as possible. Place in a large heavy pot. Add carrots, parsnips, onions, celery, and a small amount of water; cook, *not browning,* over moderate heat for 8 to 10 minutes. Add garlic, wine, lemon juice, salt and pepper to taste, and enough water to cover bones and vegetables. Reduce temperature and simmer for 3 to 4 hours. Strain mixture, return liquid to pot, and continue cooking until liquid is reduced to 2 cups. Remove from heat, stir in cream and egg yolks. Adjust seasoning, if desired. Strain again through cheese cloth or fine wire mesh sieve. If a stiffer sauce is required, stir 1 to 2 tablespoons, unflavored gelatin into sauce. Use for coating foods when temperature of sauce is lukewarm and can be brushed onto food with a pastry brush.

Madeira Sauce

Yield: two cups

6 black peppercorns
1 medium carrot, peeled and minced
1/2 medium onion, peeled and minced
1/2 celery rib, peeled and minced
2 tablespoons butter or margarine, melted
2 tablespoons flour
1 bay leaf, crumbled
1 cup beef stock or broth
1/2 cup dry red wine
1/2 cup Madeira wine
Salt and pepper to taste
1/2 tablespoon butter or margarine, at room temperature

In a medium heavy saucepan, sauté the first 4 ingredients in melted butter over moderate heat until vegetables are lightly browned. Sprinkle mixture with flour, mixing well. Add bay leaf, beef stock, and wines; cover and cook over moderate heat until vegetables are very tender. Skim pan as needed. Add salt and pepper. Strain sauce through a fine strainer or sieve; return to pan and swirl in remaining 1/2 tablespoon soft butter.

Horseradish Cream

Yield: about one cup

1/2 cup heavy cream, chilled
2 tablespoons prepared, or 2 to 3 teaspoons freshly grated horseradish
Salt and pepper to taste
Several grains cayenne pepper

In a chilled deep small bowl, beat cream with chilled beaters until stiff peaks are formed.

Fold in hoseradish, salt, pepper, and cayenne pepper.

Glazing Aspic

Yield: two and one half cups

2 cups chicken broth, divided
3 egg whites
2 ounces (8 envelopes) unflavored gelatin

In a medium heavy saucepan, combine a small amount of broth with egg whites, whisking lightly with a wire whisk. Gradually whisk in gelatin. Add remaining broth, blending well. Bring mixture to a boil, stirring constantly, over moderate heat; reduce temperature to simmer and allow mixture to simmer, unstirred, for 30 minutes. Cool and then strain before using.
Glazing: Melt aspic over low heat; transfer to a stainless steel bowl and stir to a heavy cream consistency. With a ladle or pastry brush, coat product to be glazed with aspic as desired. If aspic becomes too thick, remelt and continue glazing as previously directed.

Court Bouillon

Yield: about six cups

Bones and heads of 5 to 6 white-fleshed non-oily fish (see note)
8 black peppercorns
4 lemon slices
3 parsley sprigs
2 bay leaves, broken
8 cups water (see note)
2 cups coarsely chopped celery
1 1/2 cups coarsely chopped peeled onions
1 cup coarsely chopped peeled carrots
1/2 cup white wine vinegar
1 1/2 teaspoons minced fresh or 1/2 teaspoon dried thyme
Salt to taste

In a large heavy saucepan, combine all ingredients. Bring to a boil over moderate heat; reduce temperature and simmer, uncovered, for 1 hour, or until flavor is substantial. Strain liquid through a fine sieve, cool, and store in the refrigerator or freezer until ready to use.

Note: Use flounder, white fish, perch, sea trout, cod, haddock or other firm-fleshed non-oily fish. Do not use blue, salmon, tuna, or other oily fish.

Note: Add additional water if necessary.

How To "Turn" Vegetables

Using a sharp paring knife, round the vegetable at the edge trying to a-chieve smoothness. Place the vegetable between the thumb and forefinger of one hand; holding the paring knife in the other hand, start from the top and cut around the vegetable slowly. Continue the process until all the sides are rounded and smooth.

After the vegetables have been turned, cook them in boiling salted water until tender but crisp. For more tender veg-etables, cook for an additional few minutes, as desired. Drain vegetables and immediately im-merse in ice water to prevent vegetables from cooking fur-ther and to retain their fresh color. The vegetable may also be sautéed with butter and seasoned with a pinch of sugar and pepper.

Wheat Bread

*A visually attractive bread basket is essential
to complete a well appointed buffet table.*

Yield: two loaves or about six dozen rolls, or bread sticks

2 cups warm water (105 to 115 degrees F.)
2 ounces (cakes) compressed yeast, or 2 packages active dry yeast
2 tablespoons sugar
1 tablespoon salt
About 7 to 8 cups sifted flour, divided
Water as needed for brushing dough
Sesame or poppy seeds as desired
Coarse salt as desired

In a large bowl, combine the first 4 ingredients, blending well. Stir in 3 cups flour, beating thoroughly. Add remaining flour, 1/2 cup at a time, to make a stiff dough. Turn out onto a lightly floured board and knead until smooth and elastic. Place in a greased bowl and turn once to coat surfaces. Cover and let rise in a warm place (85 degrees F.) away from drafts, until doubled in bulk, about 1 to 1 1/2 hours. Punch down, turn out onto a lightly floured board, and shape into two loaves. Place on greased baking sheets or in greased 9x5x3-inch loaf pans. Cover and let rise again in a warm place (85 degrees F.) until doubled in bulk, about 1 hour. Or, shape into round rolls, about 3 to 4 inches in diameter, or 4-inch bread sticks, about 1/8 to 1/4-inch in width; arrange on greased baking sheets, 4 inches apart. Cover, and let rise until doubled in bulk. Brush tops of loaves or rolls or breadsticks lightly with water. Sprinkle each liberally with sesame or poppy seeds or coarse salt as desired. Bake in the lower third of a hot oven (400 degrees F.) for about 30 to 35 minutes or until done and well browned. (Bread will give a hollow sound when thumped with the forefinger). Bake rolls or breadsticks for about 15 minutes or until done.

Bread "Baskets" With Vegetables

A woven bread "basket" may be used to present a variety of vegetables, cooked meats, poultry, fish or shellfish. The dough is rolled into long sausages and woven around the wooden skewers. Use a round slice of bread for the base of the basket. Use vegetables that are blemish-free to ensure the final product being appetizing.

Crêpes

*We owe the delicate thin pancake known as the crêpe to the French.
Crêpes may be served as an hors d'oeuvre, light entrée, or dessert.*

Yield: 18 crêpes

1 1/2 cups sifted
  flour
3 tablespoons sugar
1/2 teaspoon salt
4 eggs
1 1/4 cups milk
  (approximate)
3/4 cup half-and-half
  or light cream
2 tablespoons
  brandy (optional)
Melted butter
  as needed

Sift together the first 3 ingredients. In a medium bowl, beat eggs until very light. Stir in milk, half and half, and dry ingredients, Add brandy and beat until smooth.

To make crêpes, preheat and lightly grease a 5 or 6-inch crêpe or omelet pan or skillet. Pour in 2 to 3 tablespoons of batter all at once. Tilt pan quickly and rotate to distribute batter evenly over surface. Cook the crêpe quickly on both sides. Remove crêpe from pan and brush lightly with melted butter. Repeat until all batter is used. Stack cakes and cover with a towel to keep warm.

Note: Crêpes are time-consuming to make. The above recipe can be made in advance. Foil or plastic wrap may be placed between each crêpe. The crêpes may then be frozen. To re-heat, drop thawed crêpes, one at a time, into a lightly buttered pan. Cook over moderate heat until warm, turning once.

Chocolate "Hedgehog" (Porcupine)

Yield: one "hedgehog" cake

8 ounces bittersweet chocolate
1 cup butter or margarine, at room temperature
1 1/4 cups sifted confectioners' sugar
10 large eggs, at room temperature and separated
1 teaspoon vanilla extract
1/2 cup sugar
Pinch of salt
1 1/2 cups sifted flour
Ganache Chocolate
Slivered blanched almonds
1/4 cup whipped cream
Marzipan, as needed (see note)
1 wooden pick

Melt bittersweet chocolate over boiling water; cool. In a very large bowl, cream butter thoroughly. Gradually add confectioners' sugar, beating until light and fluffy. Add cooled chocolate, mixing well. In a separate bowl, beat egg yolks until thick. Add egg yolks and vanilla to chocolate mixture, beating well. In a large bowl, combine egg whites and salt; beat until soft peaks are formed. Gradually add remaining 1/2 cup sugar, beating until stiff, but not dry, peaks are formed. Sprinkle flour over chocolate mixture; blend well. Fold in beaten egg whites, mixing until no whites streaks remain. Carefully fill a pastry/piping bag fitted with a plain nozzle with cake batter; pipe a large mound-shape to resemble the body of a "hedgehog" or "porcupine" on a sheet of ungreased parchment paper placed on a baking sheet (this process may need to be done in two or three stages, depending upon the size of the pastry/piping bag). Bake in a preheated moderate oven (375 degrees F.) for 15 minutes, or until a cake tester inserted in the cake comes out clean. Cool thoroughly on a wire rack. Cut cake vertically into thirds. Liberally spread the cut-end surfaces of the center section of cake with Ganache Chocolate, replace end sections to reform the whole mound on a serving platter and chill in the refrigerator for 1 hour. Poke slivered almonds over the whole mound of cake to resemble the quills of a "hedgehog" or "porcupine" leaving a vacant area for the "face". Cover the "face" with marzipan. With an iced tea spoon, form two dots of whipped cream to resemble the eyes and then add a dot of Gananche Chocolate to the white of each "eye" and for the "nose".

Note: Marzipan is available in specialty food stores or the gourmet sections of many grocery stores. A candied red or green cherry may be substituted for the marzipan.

Fresh Fruit Tart (Cake)

This visually appealing dessert is equally as good tasting. The sponge cake base is a version of the centuries old Continental Savoy cake. In Europe, it is often referred to as a tart. Light and airy, it uses stiffly beaten egg yolks and whites for leavening, ensuring a delicate texture. Seasonal fresh fruits and flavored sweetened whipped cream complete its composition.

Yield: one tart

6 extra large or jumbo eggs, divided and at room temperature
1/3 cup plus 1/4 cup sugar, divided
1/2 teaspoon vanilla extract (optional)
1/2 teaspoon lemon extract (optional)
1 cup sifted cake flour
About 1 to 1 1/2 cups apricot jam
Assorted seasonal fresh fruits as desired (about 2 to 3 sliced peeled or unpeeled peaches, pears, nectarines, 4 to 6 sliced peeled kiwi, or 1 pint berries of choice)
About 1 cup apricot or apple jelly
Flavored sweetened whipped cream (optional)

In a medium bowl, beat egg yolks until foamy. Gradually add 1/3 cup sugar and vanilla or lemon extract, as desired; continue beating until mixture is thick and light yellow in color. Add flour, mixing well. In a large bowl, beat egg whites until they are foamy. Gradually add remaining 1/4 cup sugar, beating until stiff, but not dry, peaks are formed. Carefully fold egg yolk mixture into beaten egg whites. Spoon batter into an ungreased 10 to 12-inch round layer pan. Bake in a moderate oven (350 degrees F.) for about 15 minutes or until cake tester inserted in the center of the cake comes out clean. Cool in pan for 3 to 4 minutes and then turn out onto a wire rack to cool thoroughly. Spread cake layer with apricot jam. Arrange fruits of choice over apricot jam. Peel and slice peaches, pears, nectarines, or kiwi. Hull and cut strawberries in half or thinly slice as desired. Use other berries of choice whole. With a pastry brush, glaze fruits with apricot or apple jelly. Garnish tart with flavored sweetened whipped cream, if desired.

Pastry Tartlettes

Black or green olives, cherry tomatoes, quail eggs, sweet or savoury jams or jellies, corn kernels, chopped red bell pepper, any flavor mousse, or many varieties of small foodstuffs can be used as fillings for tartlettes. The same pastry recipe and method of preparation are used for round or oval-shaped pastries. Oval tartlettes are used as garnishes, often filled with capers or olives or turned vegetables. Even a mousse composed of a meat base or a creamy pâté can become tartlette fillings to garnish an entrée of roast chicken or wild game.

Yield: about 6 to 8 tartlettes

1 1/2 cups sifted flour
Pinch of salt
1/4 cup butter, at room temperature
1/4 cup margarine, at room temperature
1 to 2 tablespoons ice water
1/2 tablespoon beaten egg yolk
Filling of choice

In a medium bowl, combine flour and salt. With a pastry blender, cut in butter and margarine until mixture resembles coarse meal. *Do not overmix.* Add egg yolk and enough water to hold pastry together, tossing lightly with a fork. Form into a ball. Cover and allow to rest for 20 minutes in a cool area. Roll out the dough on a lightly floured surface to a 1/8-inch thickness. Invert a 2 1/2 to 3-inch tart pan on crust and cut a circle 1 inch larger than pan; fit crust into pan. Or cut rolled pastry into 5-inch circles and fit over inverted custard cups or muffin pans. Pinch crust together, making pleats in pastry so it will sit snugly. Prick crust over sides and bottom of tart shell with tines of a dinner fork. Arrange on a baking sheet and bake in a preheated hot oven (425 degrees F.) for 8 to 10 minutes, or until lightly browned. Cool thoroughly. Fill as desired.

Cream Puffs (Pâté À Choux)

Cream puffs are called choux in France, their country of origin.
They were named for their resemblance, when baked, to miniature cabbages.
A round, airy cake, they may be filled with cream or ice cream
or served as an appetizer with a meat, egg, or shellfish filling.

Yield: fifty miniature cream puffs

1 cup water
1/2 cup butter
  or margarine
1 teaspoon sugar
3/4 teaspoon salt
1 cup sifted flour
4 large eggs
French Cream
  Filling

Combine water, butter, sugar, and salt in a small heavy saucepan; bring to a full rolling boil. Reduce heat to moderate. Add flour, all at once, stirring vigorously until mixture leaves the pan and forms a stiff ball. Remove from heat. Add eggs, one at a time, beating until mixture is smooth, shiny, and *very stiff* after each addition. Drop rounded tablespoonfuls of dough, 2 1/2-inches apart, onto ungreased baking sheets. Bake in a hot preheated oven (425 degrees F.) for 20 to 30 minutes or until puffed, golden brown, and dry. Prick puffs with the point of a knife to allow the steam to escape. Cool away from drafts. Cut off tops, remove any soft dough and fill.

French Cream Filling

Yield: about 3 1/2 cups

1 cup heavy cream,
  chilled
1/2 cup sifted con-
  fectioners' sugar
1 egg white, stiffly
  beaten
Pinch of salt
1/2 teaspoon of de-
  sired flavoring ex-
  tract such as
  vanilla, rum, or li-
  queur of choice
  (optional)

In a chilled deep small bowl, beat cream with chilled beaters, gradually adding sugar until mixture forms stiff peaks. Fold in remaining ingredients. Cover and chill until ready to use.

Garnishing Paste

Yield : 1 1/2 cups of paste

3 egg whites at
  room temperature
1 3/4 cups sugar
3 tablespoons
  lemon juice
Food color of choice

In a deep bowl, beat the egg whites into the lemon juice until egg whites are foamy; gradually add sugar, beating until stiff, but not dry, peaks are formed. Divide the paste into 2 bowls. Add a few drops of food coloring of choice to each bowl, fold color into beaten egg whites with quick short strokes. Fill a pastry/piping bag fitted with a nozzle of choice with Garnishing Paste; decorate as desired.

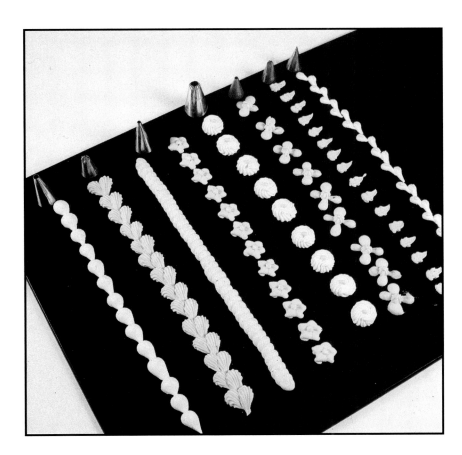

Glossary of Cooking Utensils

Apple corer...*a small device with a metal serrated edge shaped like a ring used to core apples.*

Brushes...*assorted sizes used for applying glaze to foodstuffs.*

Butter curler...*a device that curls butter and gives it a zig-zag appearance.*

Citrus Scorer/caneller cutter/channel knife...*a device with a slotted blade used to cut grooves or remove strips of peel or zest from citrus fruits and other foodstuffs.*

Cocktail and wooden/picks, with and without paper frills...*these may be purchased in any supermarket and are excellent for finger canapés, and securing a variety of foods.*

Fluted knives...*create a waffled slice of butter, carrots, turnips, jelly, aspic, etc., leaving a ruffled surface.*

Fruit or vegetable peeler...*a slotted bladed cutting device with which to remove the peel from vegetables, fruits, and other foodstuffs.*

Grapefruit knife...*a serrated, thin-bladed knife which can be used to easily cut sections from a grapefruit or orange half.*

Mandoline...*manual slicing device used to make various cuts from vegetables; i.e. ripple-cut, julienne, slices, etc.*

Paring knife...*short-bladed, short-handled knife with many uses (it is not cumbersome). A 2/3-inch to 4/5-inch blade is desirable.*

Parisian scoop or melon baller...*one or two different sized scoops mounted on opposite ends of a stainless steel or wooden handle, used for making fruit and vegetable balls.*

Pastry piping tube/bag...*funnel shaped container for holding soft food (mashed potatoes, whipped cream, cake frosting) from which the foods are forced through the pastry tube at the top to make ornamental coatings or decorations.*

Potato nest basket...*to make a nest of fried potato, a special frying basket made of steel wire is required. These are available in any kitchen shop, or two Chinese frying spoons may be used.*

Glossary of Cooking Terms

Al dente . . . *usually applied to pasta or vegetables which are slightly undercooked so they are crunchy or have some resilience to the bite.*

Aspic jelly . . . *the strained, clarified jelly made from a calf's foot or the bones of meat, fish, or poultry that solidifies when cold. The jelly may be used to mold or coat cold meat, vegetables, fish, or poultry, or to garnish same. It can be flavored with such wines as port, sherry, marsala, madeira, or white wine, or champagnes.*

Blanch . . . *to heat briefly in boiling water or steam. This procedure can be applied to fruit, vegetables, or meats.*

Blend . . . *to mix together thoroughly two or more ingredients.*

Canapé . . . *appetizer consisting of food spread on edible bases, usually bread, and then garnished.*

Chemise . . . *to glaze.*

Chaud Froid . . . *a jellied sauce composed of butter, flour, egg yolk, stock, cream and gelatin. It is used as a white glaze to cover such foods as vegetables, poultry or meats. Food covered with a chaud-froid sauce usually has been molded into shapes after cooking and is served cold. It may be white, brown, green (asparagus), or red (tomatoes).*

Coulis . . . *a pureé of fresh fruits or vegetables.*

Croquette . . . *chopped or ground food usually held together with a thick sauce, shaped and rolled in breadcrumbs or cornmeal, and fried in a skillet in deep fat or oven-baked.*

Crêpe . . . *small thin pancake of French origin filled with a variety of foodstuffs to serve as appetizers, entreés, or desserts.*

Duxelles . . . *a mixture of finely chopped mushrooms and onions, sometimes mixed with ham. It can be used raw, or cooked in butter until tender but not browned, to stuff or to flavor or to garnish another food.*

Farce . . . *a mixture of meat, poultry, vegetables, or fish used as a stuffing.*

Fleurons . . . *small cut of pastry, usually half-moon in shape.*

Feuilletes . . . *puff pastry cases (receptacles) cut into different shapes.*

Garnish . . . *mostly an edible decoration added to savoury and sweet dishes to improve appearance, to awaken tastes, and to add variety and color.*

Garniture . . . *garnish or trimming. Interesting shapes of vegetables, pastry, pasta or other small foodstuffs used to enhance the appearance and flavor of a dish.*

Gelatin . . . *colorless, tasteless, brittle substance made by boiling bones, hooves, and animal tissues. When granulated or powdered, gelatin is used to make jelly-like dishes such as aspic, desserts, molded salads, and mousses. Because gelatin has no flavor of its own, it makes a compatible ingredient for flavorful food combinations.*

Gelée . . . *jelly or jellied.*

Glâce de Viande . . . *concentrated meat glaze prepared by boiling brown stock until it is reduced in amount and thick in consistency.*

Glaze . . . *a liquid preparation (as sugar syrup, gelatin dissolved in meat stock) brushed over food (as meat, fish, pastry), which, after application, becomes firm and adds flavor and a glossy appearance.*

Herbs . . . *cultivated plants that are combined with foods to improve flavor. Some, such as parsley, basil, and chervil, can be used fresh. Most can also be used when dried.*

Hors d'oeuvre . . . *refers to the first course of a meal, although the word is sometimes used to describe a selection of savoury tidbits, served with alcoholic or non-alcoholic beverages before the main meal, or in place of such, as at a cocktail buffet party.*

Julienne . . . *fine lengths (matchstick width) of vegetables, fruits, meats, poultry, etc.*

Leaf gelatin . . . *highly refined gelatin produced in thin transparent, almost colorless sheets, approximately eight sheets per ounce.*

Medallions . . . *small rounds of meat, game, or fish which are cut evenly.*

Mousse . . . *term used for various foods of a light, airy, smooth consistency. They can be prepared from savoury foods such as poultry and fish, or seafood, or they can be prepared from sweet foods such as fruits or desserts.*

Poach . . . *to cook gently in barely trembling water.*

Refresh . . . *to stop vegetables from continuing to cook and losing their color by submerging them briefly in very cold, or ice water.*

Roast . . . *to cook meat in the oven by the action of direct dry (without liquid) heat.*

Skewer . . . *to hold in place with wood or metal sticks at one or both ends of a foodstuff. Fruits, vegetables, meats, and shellfish can be threaded onto a skewer, the metal or wooden stick used to hold a foodstuff in place.*

Stock . . . *the liquid in which meat, poultry, fish, shellfish, or vegetables have been cooked.*

Timbale . . . *food cooked or served in a castle or mound shape.*

Turn . . . *technique of cutting around vegetables to make them an even size and shape and attractive in appearance.*

Whip or whipping . . . *beating rapidly to increase volume by mixing in air.*

Van Dyke . . . *a " V" shaped blade used to cut a zig-zag edge.*

Zest . . . *finely grated lemon, orange, lime, or grapefruit peel (rind).*

Index